HON

HONEST PRAYER

John Shelby Spong

Christianity for the Third Millennium
and
St. Johann Press
HAWORTH, NJ

For further educational resources exploring the ideas and issues addressed in this and other books by John Shelby Spong, contact:

Christianity for the Third Millennium
P.O. Box 69
Morristown, NJ 07963-0069
Fax: 973-540-9584
email: cmsctm@aol.com

Originally published: Seabury Press, 1973

Library of Congress Cataloging-in-Publication Data

Spong, John Shelby.
    Honest prayer / John Shelby Spong.
        p. cm.
    Originally published: New York : Seabury Press, 1972.
    Includes bibliographical references.
    ISBN 978-1-878282-18-7
        1. Prayer—Episcopal Church. 2. Christian life—Anglican
    authors. 3. Episcopal Church—Doctrines. I. Title.

BV210.3 .S76 2001
248.3'2—dc21

00-065669

Dedicated to
Marion Alston Bourne and William Henry Marmion
Two Heroes in the Christian Pilgrimage

PREFACE

In part this book presents what is my unfinished search for the meaning and power of prayer. It is the collected thoughts of one who is sure that there is more to prayer than he can comprehend. Perhaps it will raise for some more questions than it answers, although that is not its intention. My primary purpose here is simply to remove some roadblocks, some misapprehensions, some of those barriers to prayer that I believe plague the modern mind, for they have plagued me.

The book is not presented as a scholarly exegesis of the Lord's Prayer as Jesus of Nazareth originally intended it. There are many of those already available today. Rather, it is an attempt to discern the eternal truths which are expressed in that prayer and to identify those truths as they pertain to our day, although they might be expressed quite differently. Jesus lived and taught and prayed in the context of his world. But if he is to be the Lord of all history the inner truth of his life must be lived and taught and prayed in the context of our world. In order to demonstrate this fact, I have drawn heavily on my own life's experience. Hence this book will reveal my "being," and I hope will be read as a dialogue by my reader. It is truly and honestly an offering of the self that I am, a self that I have been given by him whom I call "Source of Life."

If I had to name the immediate stimulus to my writing it would be my reading of *Our Prayer* by Louis Evely. For me the experience was one of finding water in the desert. It opened doors and allowed me to crystalize my own search with my experience as a pastor and my study of the Bible. Though I have never met Evely I did send him a portion of this book early in its preparation. His response was gentle and encouraging. Perhaps some day our paths will cross. I would like that immensely. I should also add that I have found *The Lord's Prayer* by Joachim Jeremias very helpful for scholarly background.

Several people who read the manuscript, criticized it and offered suggestions were immensely helpful, especially Helene Crooks, Clifford Dowdey, Elizabeth Jane

Horton Martin, Lucy Boswell Negus, Jean Leonard LeRoy, Cyane Hoar Lowden, and Celia Kyle Luxmoore. Robert O. Kevin, retired professor of Old Testament, and Richard Reid, present professor of New Testament at my seminary, were both valued advisors; though let it be stated for their sakes that they are not responsible for my exegesis or my point of view. My staff at St. Paul's, especially the Reverend Walton Speake Pettit and Diane Murray Snow, were patient with my absences and the increased workload they had to bear; so also was my congregation who gave me the time to do the work.

From the inception of this book to the very end of its preparation, my wife, Joan, and my daughters, Ellen, Katharine, and Jaquelin, have made it all worthwhile, for from them I draw my greatest love and strongest support. My hope is that they might say the same of me.

JOHN SHELBY SPONG

Richmond, Virginia
May, 1972

CONTENTS

HONEST PRAYER

And now, as our Saviour Christ hath taught us,
*   we are bold to say,*
Our Father, who art in heaven,
Hallowed be thy Name.
Thy kingdom come.
Thy will be done,
On earth as it is in heaven.
Give us this day our daily bread.
And forgive us our trespasses,
    As we forgive those who trespass against us.
And lead us not into temptation,
    But deliver us from evil.
For thine is the kingdom,
    and the power, and the glory,
    for ever and ever. Amen.
                    —The Book of Common Prayer

*And in praying do not heap up empty phrases as the Gentiles do;
for they think that they will be heard for their many words. Do
not be like them, for your Father knows what you need before
you ask him. Pray then like this:*

Our Father who art in heaven,
Hallowed be thy Name.
Thy kingdom come,
Thy will be done,
  On earth as it is in heaven.
Give us this day our daily bread;
And forgive us our debts,
  As we also have forgiven our debtors;
And lead us not into temptation,
  But deliver us from evil.
            —Matthew 6:7–13 RSV

And he said to them, When you pray say:
Father, hallowed be thy Name. Thy kingdom come. Give us each
day our daily bread; and forgive us our sins, for we ourselves forgive every one who is indebted to us; and lead us not into temptation.   —Luke 11:2–4 RSV

Our Father in heaven,
  holy be your Name,
  your kingdom come,
  your will be done,
    on earth as in heaven.
Give us today our daily bread.
Forgive us our sins
  as we forgive those who sin against us.
Do not bring us to the test
  but deliver us from evil.
For the kingdom, the power,
    and the glory are yours
  now and for ever. Amen.
         —*Services for Trial Use, 1971*

CHAPTER 1

Difficulties Encountered in Praying

→⟫-⟫ P R A Y E R has always had for me a magnetic attraction. I have never been without it, and yet I have also found myself unable to discuss it in glib categories or self-assured words. At one and the same time I am drawn by its power and repelled by its form. I live in the ambiguous contradiction of the ordained minister called upon to pray in a myriad of circumstances, and yet I am not certain how I feel about the effectiveness of the standard words and forms of traditional prayer.

This contradiction has always been a part of my life. While a seminary student, I could be deeply moved by theology, biblical studies, and the power of that Christian community. Yet my attempts to develop a meaningful prayer life seemed always to come to naught. Indeed I was, as Bishop Robinson suggests in his book *Honest to God,* one who lived under the guilt of inadequacy when I compared the meaning I *found* in prayer with the meaning I felt I was *supposed* to find there. I recall vividly that on those days set aside for meditation at the seminary, I found myself bored beyond endurance. Invariably, I would end those quiet days sound asleep in an overstuffed chair in the basement of the library. Later, in my attempts to overcome this deficiency, I imposed upon myself every prayer discipline imaginable; but none of them really worked for me. I read the devotional classics of the ages; they never quite talked about my world. I continued to feel the burden of what I call "prayer inadequacy" and, driven by this burden, I went on reading every new book on the subject I could find.

Few of these books were of any help. They were either very religious, presenting God in all of his transcendent power but without any connection with my life, or they were folksy, the random thoughts of a man driving on a freeway, quite unrelated to that Power I call the biblical God.

Furthermore, the very form of prayer presented by these religious-type books, while using all the traditional Christian words, portrayed a kind of Christianity that was alien to my faith and the experiences of my life. And

I just could not become the spiritual master, director of souls, or school-of-prayer leader they seemed to suggest that I ought to be.

Neither were the new secular prayers of any help to me, for they seemed to eliminate the transcendent in their search for relevance. That kind of one-dimensional conversation with oneself did not do justice to the great experiences of reality that I have known inside the Christian faith. To me they appeared to be a secular protest to an irrelevant Christianity, but one which offered no alternative of substance. It was like the smile of the Cheshire cat that remained after the cat had disappeared.

Yet the ministry of the Christian Church thrilled and excited every fiber of my being. I felt the transforming power of God in all kinds of relationships. In my pastoral contacts with many people facing serious crises, there was meaningful sharing that significantly expanded my life and, I hope, their lives. Time after time in such moments I found the words and symbols of the Christian faith illumining these experiences. This was to me undeniable reality. Still, however, prayer in its traditional form did not add a new dimension to these relationships; nor did it seem to make contact with any experience in which I was discovering life or meaning. It did not grip me or my world with interpretive power. Yet prayer had been for so long a significant part of that religious heritage in which I stand that I could not simply dismiss it. I wanted to pray, but I wanted that prayer to be honest and real. No pattern or form of prayer known to me allowed this combination of honesty and meaning. So I remained and still am a seeker. I affirm with all my being that this truth and reality is to be found in prayer despite my inability to locate the key. This unresolved conflict has served to keep me passionately interested in the subject of prayer.

The more deeply I probed this matter of prayer, the more I realized that my primary problem rested with the traditional forms and was twofold: first, the language of prayer baffled me; and second, the theological concepts undergirding traditional prayer patterns were contrary to my understanding of the Christian faith. Both aspects of the problem needed to be dealt with before I could begin to discover prayer and its meaning.

When I refer to the language of prayer, I do not mean words, the simple problem of word changes over the centuries or even the "thee" and "thou" of Elizabethan English. As a matter of fact, I enjoy the Elizabethan "sounds of worship." But I do mean, rather, the language of prayer that is at worst superstitious and at best nonsensical. It was Louis Evely in his exciting book, *Our Prayer,* who first articulated for me this vague discontent. He encouraged me to think rationally about the meaning of many prayer phrases I had used uncomfortably for years, phrases such as "Lord have mercy upon us," "Remember thy servant," "The Lord be with you," and many, many more.

What does it mean to beseech God to have mercy? Is

it not the nature of God to be merciful? Do our prayers make him more so? Is not the prayer "Lord have mercy," a case of our asking God to be what he already is? But can he be less than what he is? Does not this prayer really intend to ask that *our* lives might be kept open to the mercy of the God whose name is Love? If that is our prayer, then why do our words say something quite different?

Similarly, the phrase "The Lord be with you," which is so familiar in our worship tradition, is also filled with difficulty. This phrase seems to assume that there are times when God is not with us so that we need to request his presence. But certainly the Christian revelation portrays an omnipresent power of life and love we call by the holy name, God. We may not always be aware of his presence, but it is his nature to be ever present. What, then, do the words of our prayer mean? Are we trying to say "The Lord is with you" in order to call people's lives and minds to a conscious awareness of the Source of their life and being? If that is our intent, then why does not the language of prayer reflect it?

How often do we hear ministers, in both liturgical and nonliturgical churches, beseech God, "Remember thy servant"? One gets the impression that many of us fear that God has amnesia and that his memory is not trustworthy. It is as if our prayer is to recall him to his duty, to remind him to be what he is. Yet is this not at heart a petition that we be assured that we are not alone in the vastness of the universe, but that our lives are grounded in that which transcends our finitude? Then why cannot our words say what we mean?

The more I analyzed the traditional words of our worship, the more the language presented a barrier to me, and the more I began to understand why I felt so ill at ease with the classic forms of prayer. This led me to define clearly what meaningful prayer is *not*. It is not an attempt to call God to his duties. Our situation in prayer is not one of a child asking an authority for a favor, nor of a beggar on his knees beseeching a master for a crumb. Yet time after time, in our attitudes and, indeed, even in our posture, we portray this image. It is no wonder that this form of prayer is abandoned today by so many or that prayer has become for numerous modern men and women a veritable "forgotten language."

Yet I know that many well-meaning, religious people who hear or read these things will suggest that I am destroying the very justification of and need for prayer. When I say, as I believe, that no prayer of man can change God's will, his life, or his nature, many will misunderstand me and assume that I am saying that prayer is ineffective, and hence we need to pray no longer. But is our problem with prayer located in God, or is it, rather, in our lives and world, which have moved so far from God's intention for creation? If God's will is perfection, it can only be changed by making it less than perfect. Is it our desire in prayer to destroy God by bending his will to ours? Sometimes our prayers seem to say just that.

But suppose the focus of prayer is not God at all, but the one who is praying. Suppose prayer is the means whereby we open this broken and distorted world with its specific broken and hurting lives to the perfect and healing will of God. Suppose our prayers offer God a channel through which to work that might not otherwise be open to him. Suppose the act of prayer is one way, in God's grace, that we participate in the divine work of creation and redemption. Then perhaps we will grasp the enormous necessity of prayer. Prayer does not "work" on God. If it did, we should have little or no praying to do. Prayer "works" on the one who prays, the one for whom he prays, and the world for which he prays. It could be, then, that the traditional language of prayer has the order exactly backward. Prayer is the activity through which God reaches man and not the activity through which man reaches God. I believe this must have been St. Paul's insight when he wrote: "The Spirit in us utters things too deep for words" (Romans 8:26).

When I turn from the language problem to the theological problem, I find the difficulties of prayer only heightened. The form of prayer which has dominated Christian history was shaped by the monastic movement. This movement expressed a life-denying, other-worldly mentality that is quite foreign to the Bible. The monks of the early church were much imbued with a dualistic Neoplatonism that caused them to divide reality into two realms. The physical or material realm they saw as evil. The nonphysical, or "spiritual," realm they viewed

as good. Hence their prayers tended to be escapist, pietistic, and increasingly unreal. So divorced from real life
was the discipline of prayer that the ordinary Christian
of the Middle Ages was quite content to let the monks
do his praying for him. He would tip his hat in recognition of the need for prayer by occasionally going on a
retreat or a pilgrimage, but he did not think real prayer
was, or could be, his personal vocation. The medieval
prayer pattern was built on the assumption that God was
found beyond life. Prayer, thought of as an approach
to God, became through the example of the monastic
communities an attempt to escape life, time, and the
world, since God could not be found in these spheres.
The monastic mode of prayer was to turn away from
life, to shut out the world, to soar to the realm of the
spirit. The final reward of prayer was not a transformed
world, but a beatific vision. When one reads the traditional books on prayer, one finds this their basic attitude.

But this attitude is deeply incompatible with the
Christian faith I have been taught and to which I am
committed. To the biblical mind, God was the Creator
of his world, the Power of history, the inescapable Presence of life. When the Hebrews looked for God, they
did not try to shut out the world, but instead they found
God in life and in history. By medieval, or even modern
standards, it is quite difficult to find a pietistic otherworldly Hebrew. God, to the biblical mind, was a Force
with which to reckon, a Power to be engaged, a Reality

to be experienced. To have faith, for the Hebrew, was not to do some mental activity like believing; it was, rather, to possess the ability to enter life expectantly, confident that God was there to be found. To be open to God's revelation for the Hebrew was to have faith, and this faith produced in one the courage to be.

Nowhere is this better seen than in the cycle of Abraham stories (Genesis 12–25). These stories come chiefly from the pen of the Yahwist writer who wrote near the end of the reign of Solomon. He created his saga about the founding father of Israel from fragments of history, myth, and folklore. Inevitably, he portrayed in Abraham the qualities that he felt marked the Hebrew nation. Abraham was a wanderer, a stranger, called by God out of the security of his past into an unknown future, an unknown tomorrow. He left his ties with family, clan, and home to set out in a new direction, trusting only the promise of God, which was twofold: that he was to possess a promised land and that he was to be the father of a great people. In the Abraham story that promise is threatened time after time. The land which he was promised was held by the Canaanites; and the wife through whom the child of promise was to come was barren. Yet still Abraham trusted. Still he walked forward into tomorrow and entered life expectantly: "By faith Abraham obeyed . . . and he went out not knowing where he was to go" (Hebrews 11:8).

Biblical prayer reveals this life-centered assumption time and again. Biblically, if one wanted to search for

God, one had to turn toward life, toward history. To walk before God was to walk into the future of the world. Examine the prayers of Jeremiah or Job. Penetrate the substance of prayer in the Book of Psalms. Biblical prayer was *engagement* with life, not *disengagement* from life. Holiness was found in life, not outside life. The world was the creature of God, not the realm of evil materialism. History was the arena in which revelation was received, and it must be entered to find God. Prayer must be an approach to life if it is to be an approach to God.

It was only when Christianity left its Hebrew origins and began to think in the Neoplatonic concepts of the ancient world that this other-worldly confusion began to affect the Christian prayer experience, for the Neoplatonists had separated the realm of God from the realm of the world. When this dualistic assumption of the Neoplatonic mind became the dominant concept of Christian theology, the monastic prayer pattern was possible. Thus Christian prayer came to be defined by dualistic-thinking mystics, holy men, and spiritualists. They are the ones who began to write prayer manuals, prayer rules of life, and prayer disciplines, all of which were designed to help us escape the evils of our world and become "spiritual." This is what has created for us the classic form of prayer. But as a Christian I cannot make these assumptions nor can I practice these prayer forms with their retreats, quiet days, and prayer disciplines which are based upon these assumptions.

I am not alone in this experience.

As long as men were convinced that this realm of the spirit was both real and important, this monastic pattern of prayer survived. Those who continue to find meaning in these patterns today do so because the realm of the spirit still has reality for them. I do not criticize them so much as I envy them. But let us admit that this old-fashioned certainty is a luxury that few people in our age can enjoy. The realm of the "spirit" is quite suspect today. This is not the late Middle Ages, although many religious writers seem to wish it were.

The "spiritual" world was the dominant reality until the thirteenth or fourteenth century. Life here was robbed of its meaning, and all attention was focused on the life to come. All art was religious art, for no other subject was of sufficient worth to merit artistic talent. All music was church music, basically plainsong with its haunting melodies reflecting the struggle of the soul to escape life here for life there. Human life was defined as an immortal soul incarcerated in a fleshly, and there-fore evil, body of which someday it would be free. Any study of physical reality was deemed unworthy of a Christian mind; hence there was little scientific en-deavor, and whenever there was, the church tended to frown upon it. Any attempt at social reform was con-sidered a waste of time, for this world was so insignificant that it did not merit reform. People were taught to ac-cept their status, "and to do my duty in whatever state it shall please God to call me" (Offices of Instruction,

Book of Common Prayer). Moreover, there was no passion to prolong life. The status of the medical doctor
was quite low, for no great value was laid on saving life
when so great a home as heaven awaited Christians.
Here on this earth human beings were strangers or pil-
grims. Heaven was their destiny, their true dwelling
place, and prayer was the means through which they
kept contact with that spiritual realm. Life was to be
punctuated by meditations designed to transport the
Christian heavenward. Prayer life could range from
long periods of retreat to momentary flights of "arrow
prayers" that Christians hurled heavenward in order
to keep touch with that which they conceived alone to
be real.

But these thought forms are not part of our contemporary life. It is easy to trace how our dilemma developed. Neoplatonic thought separated God from his
world, the spiritual from the material. Then, on the
basis of that pattern, the medieval church identified its
life and gospel almost exclusively with the realm of the
spiritual. As the church increased its dominance over
life, the spiritual realm robbed the earth-bound and
physical of any importance. God was taken out of life
and isolated in an otherworldly sphere. This development reached its zenith in the thirteenth century, when
in the thought of theology, God and the world seemed
totally separate from each other. Once God is so assigned
to a specific domain, he is inexorably tied to the fate of
that domain. Since the thirteenth century, the other-

worldly realm of the spirit has shrunk in importance and influence until today it is all but dead. Nothing will revive it. The God identified so exclusively with that realm is dead. The prayer pattern that seeks to transport us to that realm is dead. In this lies, I believe, the faith crisis of our time.

Copernicus knocked man off his pristine pedestal at the center of the universe. Darwin destroyed man's arrogance that caused him to think of himself in the analogy of "a little lower than the angels," instead of a little higher than the animals. Freud delved into man's inner life and caused him to doubt the reality of every noble thought, every heavenly vision. Marx suggested that any vision which diverted power or energy from the struggle for human justice here and now was a vile delusion or a deliberate opiate. With these modifications of outlook we entered the twentieth century.

Our day can be characterized as a thirteenth century-in-reverse. Today this world is the all-encompassing, powerful reality. Heaven is considered a pleasant illusion. Science is king! Theology is thought of as being for those who "like that sort of thing." Today this life is so important and so final that social reform for now, not tomorrow is a passion. The modern man or woman is this-world centered, life-centered, pragmatic, scientifically oriented. He or she does not understand or respond to the escapism of medieval spirituality.

Yet the church still presents the matter of prayer in a medieval guise. Modern man is urged to turn in prayer to the realm of the spirit. Most do not turn. The man or woman who does finds little or no meaning there. The words of a religious ritual have a phony ring in his ear when he seriously scrutinizes them with his mind. Since no other prayer pattern is presented, it is no wonder that contemporary man ceases to pray. It is obvious that when he ceases to pray or when prayers become empty forms and meaningless words, God grows dim and that he as a man feels increasingly alone in the universe. If such a person wants to continue his church affiliation, he carefully avoids thinking or raising questions about prayer, or he persists in childhood prayer patterns because of the warm emotional feelings associated with the familiar "Now I Lay Me Down to Sleep," for instance.

Traditional Christianity does not offer the modern person a very meaningful alternative. He can follow the monastic prayer pattern and become, inevitably, a pietist, an escapist; or he can refuse to accept that pattern and become a materialist. If he finds no meaning except in the here and now, he will either "live it up" and become a hedonist, or battle the threat of despair and become a disciplined stoic. If the despair becomes too intense, he might even opt out of life in one of the many forms of self-negation from alcohol and drugs to suicide.

But I believe that the Christian faith must offer and *does* offer an exciting alternative to this gloomy picture, and it is to point to that new possibility that I write these words.

When the disciples asked Jesus to teach them to pray,

he responded by giving them the words of the Lord's Prayer. I believe, therefore, that this must be our starting place for any new discussion on prayer. Here in this most basic of all prayers for the Christian faith, we find in our Lord's own words some answers to our questions or at the least a new doorway through which to enter the prayer experience. But before beginning to plough that exciting and fertile field, it seems imperative that I state positively where I am in my personal quest for prayer's meaning. It is not enough merely to analyze or to be critical.

I must begin by making a simple distinction. There is in my mind a difference between "prayer" and "saying prayers." First, I define prayer in a rather traditional way. It is a human attempt to make contact with God. But God for me is found *in* life, not *beyond* life. I do not mean to state that God is not beyond life, only that we do not find him there. This is a crucial difference. For after we find him, we know that no limit can be placed on his Infinite Being. Therefore, if prayer is our attempt to discover God, prayer must be an approach to life.

The life of prayer is thus for me the responsibility to open myself in love to the transcendent in everyone I meet. It is to meet life with all that I have and all that I am. It is to be ready to encounter people, to participate in events, to live in relationships. To live the life of prayer is thus to be vulnerable. It is to run the risk of being hurt in order to love. It is to live with courage and honest involvement with my world. It is to love life as my meeting place with the Holy, my meeting place with God. J. H. Oldham wrote a book entitled *Real Life is Meeting*. Real prayer is meeting also, I am suggesting. This, I understand, is what the New Testament means when it says, "Pray without ceasing" (1 Thessalonians 5:17). Obviously, it is not referring to a ritual act; but on the contrary, to an entire way of life.

If this is prayer, what then is the meaning of saying prayers? Perhaps you ask if I engage in this activity. Let me assure you that I do, daily and specifically. I pray for those who are living in a time of stress, in sickness, death, fear. I feel that to say prayers is to unleash power, though I am not sure how it works. But I hasten to add that "saying prayers" is not a substitute for me for a human relationship. I do not go to a sick room or to the home of parishioners or even to a public meeting to say words to an uninvolved deity with uninvolved people. I go to share life with its pain, its love, its fear, its joy. I go to be what I am, a child of God. I go to call another into being what he or she is, a child of God, no matter what the present circumstances of life might be. I resent it when people will not allow me to be real and human, when I am forced to role play the praying preacher and to say "a little prayer," as they call it. I resist the expectation level that demands that I be "religious" and do the expected thing.

Saying a prayer in a shared relationship is deeply meaningful to me; but only because I have met another as a person, and we have shared and touched and experienced the Holy together. Then prayer makes that plain and obvious and real.

I pray in private daily, but these are not for me the most holy moments in an otherwise secular life. I do not use such time of prayer to have my batteries recharged or to achieve the tranquility or peace to be found only in retreat or withdrawal from life. Indeed, it is in what men call the secular life that I experience the Holy. My peace and tranquility come in my involvement with life and people. It is in life—in living, being, sharing, loving, and in honest meeting with another— that I am recharged and find peace and experience the holy God. "Saying prayers" is important in that it prepares me to meet life, to discern the Holy in life as I live. To live, for me, is to know and to be known, to love and to be loved, to forgive and to be forgiven. These are my moments of meaning. These are my times of communion with him whom I believe to be the Source of Life. These are the holy times of prayer for me. Saying prayers prepares me for this level of life, for this state of readiness and openness and expectancy. It prepares me to know the holy God when I meet him in life as I know, care, love, and share with another.

I think Jesus was talking about saying prayers when he said, "Watch ye for ye know not the day or the hour when the Son of Man comes" (Matthew 25:13).

I say prayers so that when I turn to life, I will experience and recognize the holy God *in* life, for I believe he is revealed in relationships in his world. I want my life to be lived in such an open way that it *is* a "prayer without ceasing." I want my prayers to be so honest that they proclaim the presence of the Source of Life and point my life toward his world where he is found. In this way, I believe that even for the nonmonastic, non-spiritual, but this-world-oriented modern man, prayer can be as rich and as full an experience as it has ever been in our Christian history.

From this point of view, I turn now to the prayer Jesus taught his disciples with the hope that we might learn anew to pray with honesty and say "Our Father" in this secular age.

CHAPTER 2

Addressing God as Father

→≫→≫ IN THE familiar opening phrase of the Lord's Prayer, naturally and without effort, God is addressed as "Our Father." Yet I cannot help but wonder how appropriate it is in our modern day to call him by this name. Our society has been permeated with the thought of Sigmund Freud; like it or not, we are an inward-looking, motive-searching people. We question all kinds of traditional practices. The thought of God after the analogy of father is certainly high on that list of suspect practices. Freud suggested that the idea of God was nothing more than parental authority writ large across the heavens. He envisioned the Father God as an emotional crutch on which weak and dependent people lean when they cannot face life alone. He concluded that it was a concept that perpetuates infantilism among adults who cannot grow up emotionally, who are weak and passive, and need constantly to relate to that power whom they address as "Our Father."

When this cultural Freudianism is added to the contemporary image of fatherhood in Western civilization, the concept is even more confused. The fatherhood we see illustrated in comic strips by Dagwood and Pappy Yokum or portrayed on television is that of the weak fathers of situation comedy, all of whom lack the dignity of masculinity. Television seems to know how to portray masculinity only as an unmarried, detective type or as a cowboy fighting for law and order in the Old West. We search at length to find a contemporary credible portrait of manly fatherhood. Hence to address God as "Our Father" inevitably raises more questions than it answers.

So if we are to continue to pray the Lord's Prayer, we must cut away the misconceptions today read into the word "Father" by searching out its biblical origin and use. Once we have found it, we may have to translate it some other way for our age, or at least we must allow new power to be read into its definition.

In the Old Testament the word "father" is used as a title of God only fourteen times. In most of these texts the aspects of fatherhood to which the title points are those which refer to the father's position as progenitor or founder of the family, the head of the household, or the authority who governs it—the one, therefore, to

whom honor is due. For example, we read in Deuter-
onomy (32:5–6) ". . . they are no longer his children
. . . Is he not your father, who created you, who made
you and established you?" God is the founder and, therefore, the Father of the nation. Malachi (1:6) has the same
thought in mind when he writes: "A son honors his
father, and a servant his master. If then, I am a father,
where is my honor?" However, the Hebrew word we
translate "father" in all these texts is a formal word, a
title meaning creator, deliverer, elector, protector. Hosea
could use the same concept and call it "husband" instead
of "father," and in this patriarchal society, the meaning
could be interchangeable. God as Father in this Old
Testament sense is the Power or Being beyond the life
of man, the Source of life, the One who stands against
the arrogance of human life when it asserts that man
is the measure of all things. In this Old Testament sense,
to pray to the Father was to open oneself to the transcendent Source of Life. To pray was to believe that
there is more in the universe than man sees or knows.
It was to keep human life in a proper perspective.

In the New Testament the title "father" is frequently
used. Paul, the earliest of the New Testament writers
uses it thirty-seven times. Mark, the author of the first
gospel, employs it only four times; but in Luke it appears nineteen times, and in Matthew forty-two times.
The fourth evangelist, John, makes it the all-inclusive
word for God and uses it no less than one hundred and
eleven times. The frequency of appearance, however, is
not the only difference in the two Testaments. In almost

every instance of New Testament use, the word "father" appears in some utterance of Jesus. It was above all else, his word for God. Even when Paul is using the word, it is with reference to the God "who is the father of Jesus" or to our relationship with this father God whom we have in Jesus. If we are to understand "Father" in its New Testament sense, we must see then what it meant to Jesus, for he is the one who established it as the unique name for God, and the word he used was filled with new, subtle, and different meanings.

The overwhelming evidence is that the Aramaic word for Father used by Jesus was *Abba,* an intensely personal and intimate word that to the best of knowledge had never before been used in reference to God (Joachim Jeremias). Jesus spoke to the Father as a son, simply and securely. Yet when we look at his life, it becomes obvious that the Father Jesus knew did not delight in dangling his children on a string, puppetlike, in order to keep them subservient. He was not a Father who created dependency by making his son subject to him. He was not a Father who kept the issue of inheritance hanging over the son's head as a mechanism of control; nor was he a Father who derived ego satisfaction from being served by those over whom he had power. If a father keeps a son dependent, he can never have the son's love. Dependency breeds irritation, aggression, bondage, hostility. In the final analysis, one cannot love a person who robs him of human dignity by assigning him the status of permanent infantilism.

But look at the Father revealed through Jesus Christ. He is the Father who already has given all that he has, hence Jesus is a man who no longer expects anything of his Father—no presents, no favors. He is the Father of whom Jesus could say, "All that the Father has is mine" (John 16:15). Jesus thus could recognize in prayer that God was first of all the Giver of all things, who asked only that this giving not stop with the Son. The one who had so freely received had also to freely give. Hence, the presence of the Father was to be seen in the fullness of the life lived by the Son as the Son gave that life away. His purpose was to give of the Father's love and in the giving to restore creation and life to that which God had intended, to assist men in expressing the deepest truth about themselves—namely, that they were and are the children of God, made in the image of God, called to be what they are and to share in the creation and redemption of the world. It was out of this understanding of God that Jesus could use the intimate and lovely Aramaic word *Abba,* "dear Father."

This same powerful truth was expressed in Paul's letter to the Christians at Rome when he said that to say *"Abba—*Father" was to be not a slave but a son (Romans 8:14–17). The primary truth about a son to Paul was that he was an heir—heir to all the Father possessed. When one has been given everything, there is nothing left except giving in one's turn. The Father is one who gives all that he has; the Son is he who is the heir to all things. It is not a relationship of dominant parent to submissive child, authority to dependency, strong to weak.

As final evidence, look at the life of Jesus. Mark his strength, his security, his power, his freedom, his being. Look at his capacity to give, to care, to love. Observe his sense of his own worth and value, his dignity, and confidence. Here is a man who is whole, free, outgoing. "Father" is his word—not the word of a weak and dependent child, but the word of a man strong in his own being. So fulfilled was he that he spent his life in giving. He was open to receive and he was free to give. From the Father he had possessed his inheritance, his value, his worth, his dignity. A true father gives all that he has, including his fatherhood. God, understood as Father, gives all that he is, including his Godhood. He gives in order to call us into being all that we can be, persons who reflect the fullness of life, free men who are capable of giving to others the gifts of our life and our love. All this is in Jesus' word for God, "Father."

Perhaps in our own day, instead of the compromised word "Father," we should say, "You who give all that you are, who call us to be all that we can be, who make us heirs to all the love and power of the universe, you who expect us to give as we have received from you"— for in these words we would come close to translating what Jesus meant when he taught us to pray "Our Father." It is a prayer whose primary effect ought to be a deepening commitment to live and to be, to love, and to give of what we are to our world.

CHAPTER 3

What Does Heaven Mean Today?

→»»→»» T O T H E deeply religious generations of the past, the word "heaven" was the symbol of joy and peace, and probably was the most meaningful word in the vocabulary of religion. To the secularized nonreligious generation of today, the word "heaven" is an empty mockery, a pious dream, a false hope. One generation has placed upon this word more weight than it can possibly bear, whereas the other generation judges the word to be incapable of bearing *any* weight or meaning.

With this in mind, let us attempt to explore this word "heaven," not as that word is employed in popular religious jargon, but in its biblical origins and use; and particularly to seek its meaning on the lips of Jesus of Nazareth when he taught us to pray, "Our Father, who art in heaven."

My starting place for theological definition is always the root of our faith, the experience of the Hebrew people. Interestingly enough, in the Old Testament the primary meaning of the word "heaven" is simply "the sky," sky and heaven being almost synonymous. "The heavens declare the glory of God," declares the psalmist (Psalm 19:1). Or again, "When I consider the heavens, the works of thy hands, what is man?" (Psalm 8:3–4). The Old Testament also speaks of God who sends forth rain from heaven (1 Kings 8:35), and manna (Exodus 16:4) and dew from heaven (Genesis 27:39). Heaven meant the sky, not some otherworldly sphere where God was to be found. For to the Old Testament Hebrew mind, God was the power experienced by men in life, in the world, and in living history.

The Hebrew was never a pantheist. God was found in life, but life did not equal God. God was found in creation, but he was more than his creation. The world was his creature. We must remember that the Bible was written in pre-Copernican times. It was a world which believed literally that the created order had three tiers and that the sky was a dome over the earth, and beyond the sky was the Ultimate Power, the Source of Life, the Holy God. From the sky, the heavens, came forth the gifts of the beneficent deity and, on occasion, the acts of an angry deity in the form of natural disasters such as hurricanes, tornadoes, and heat waves. Above all, heaven, the region beyond the sky, symbolized for the Hebrew not the place where one looked for God, but the otherness of God, the transcendence of God, the fact that life had a beyond, a depth, a height, something more than that which was seen and felt and experienced in a sensory way. Only rarely in the Old Testament did being with God mean going to dwell beyond the sky. In Hebrew thought generally, God was the omnipresent, inescapable Power that one found wherever he lived: "Whither shall I go from thy Spirit? Where shall I flee from thy presence? If I ascend to heaven, thou art there. If I descend into hell, thou art there. If I take the wings of the morning and dwell in the uttermost parts of the sea; even there, thy hand shall lead me, and thy right hand shall hold me (Psalm 139:7ff.). In the Old Testament, God was met in life. Only in the strange and mysterious story of the translation of Elijah to heaven can I find the implication that one goes beyond the skies to be with God at death.

Out of Persia, however, there came another definition of heaven; based upon a different view of reality, it was disseminated by the Neoplatonists and in time gained a certain dominance in Western thought. This dualistic view divided all reality into two eternal "verities," spirit and matter; and God, who was identified as spirit, was systematically deprived of contact with the material. More and more, men believed that to be in the presence of

God was to be outside the physical world. A passion to escape life came to be equated with achieving union with God. Heaven, the symbolic word, which to the Hebrew stood for the idea that the God of life was larger than life, larger than the world, larger than creation, now was thought of as an otherworldly place, the abode of God, the place to which one went when one left this earth. When a would-be comforter tells a bereaved child not to cry for his daddy because he has gone to heaven, the primary meaning of such counsel to the child is that daddy has left him and he is alone in the world, for to be in heaven is not to be in this world. It is to be gone, to be removed, to be beyond the skies. To human experience, here and now, it is to be dead. This is the content of the word "heaven" familiar to most of us.

Our generation has been raised with this understanding, which is so different from the biblical view, and when we pray "Our Father who art in heaven," we envision a God removed from life, a God in an alien place from our world, a God shut away, otherworldly, who has retreated to a haven called heaven.

Furthermore, the farther removed heaven came to be, the less real God seemed. God was an explanation for the inexplicable. He filled in the gaps of human knowledge; what we could account for in no other way, we attributed to God. However, with each new scientific discovery the gaps became thinner and thinner, and God more and more distant, and heaven more and more unreal. Modern life began to lose all meaning, except the meaning of the here and now. Thus, there is for the contemporary man or woman no transcendence, no depth, no height, no hell, no heaven; and for so many there is, finally, no God.

In only a few places has the word "heaven" been retained in our language in a believable way. William Wordsworth has stated: "To be young was very heaven" (*The Prelude,* XI). Youth meant life, love, vitality. In the contemporary lyrics of romantic ballads, we hear a lover sing of the communion and relationship he shares with the beloved. "It's like heaven," he says. To be alive, to be loved, to be accepted, to be at one with another, to be affirmed, to be fulfilled, that is to be in heaven. Poets and lovers recognize what some theologians have forgotten: that life and love are first and primarily experienced in human relationships. They seem to sense almost intuitively the biblical truth that God is first and foremost the Source of Life, the Source of Love. Hence where love is experienced and life is lived, there God is present and there heaven is real.

I remember well an extremely difficult period of my ministry in a small, eastern North Carolina town. I was a young and brash, perhaps even hostile, clergyman who somehow had conceived of my role as that of ushering in the kingdom of God. The people, generally speaking, in that community were not at all eager to welcome the kingdom, particularly if it brought about significant changes in the power structure. I was undaunted by such opposition and, dressed in King Arthur's armor, I mounted my white horse and led the charge for righteousness.

The content of the battle was racial. School integration had just begun. The black community had awakened to new possibilities for life for which they began to press. I was naive enough to believe that as soon as I preached the truth it would be heard and people would change. I threw into the fight all the skill and power at my disposal. My sermons were brilliant masterpieces, or so I thought. My actions were bold and daring, or so I believed. But somehow the result was not what I had imagined. The people of my congregation did not seem to appreciate my scholarship and my oratory. Far from being able to change their attitudes, my judgment on them simply solidified their resistance.

Suddenly life was very lonely. I watched people cross the street in order to keep from having to speak to me. I noticed people leaving church by the side door to avoid shaking my hand. My telephone would ring late at night with anonymous threats against my family. The inevitable cross was burned. I never doubted that I was right on the issues, but I did doubt that I knew the meaning of the Gospel. For suddenly there was no community in which I could live and from which I could draw support. When my deeds failed to achieve acceptance, I discovered how deeply alienated I was from myself. The shrillness of my voice revealed an inner rejection. My harsh judgments revealed my own guilt of being, my deep-seated sense of inadequacy. External loneliness was the final outward form of internal loneliness. I had not heard the Gospel.

Then came conversion. It was not a blinding vision

or a heavenly voice. It was the hand of a friend who reached across the chasm and called me to be who I am. This friend did not agree with me on the issues, but he cared for my person. Behind him there were others, eight couples to be specific, who pulled me, with my wife, back into the life of a community. When the loneliness of estrangement is overcome by the community of love, one tastes ever so delicately the meaning of heaven.

Heaven is the presence of God. God is in the love of his people. To be loved is to be called into being. It is to be free to love and to accept oneself without bragging on the one hand, or sympathy-seeking on the other. It is to believe that one has a self worthy to share with another and thus one is free to give. It is in giving and receiving love and life that God is found and life's deepest dimensions are discovered. This is where heaven is first experienced, I believe.

Where else is the Christian God discovered but in life? Our Christian story is of the God who so loved the world that he entered it (John 3:16). Our Christ is the One who said, "I have come that you might have life" (John 10:10). It is our Lord who says the mark of the Christian is not piety, but love (John 13:35). Wherever love is shared and life is lived, there the Source of Life is known and there God is experienced. The only place the biblical God is discovered is in the midst of life, but once we know him there, we find him in life everywhere, for to meet him in life is to know that he is bigger than life, the Creative Ground of Life, the Transcendent Dimension of Life. He is the God who does not live in some otherworldly place called heaven, nor does he dwell among the religious trappings and pious platitudes of the church. The church celebrates him, worships him and points to him, but he is in the world. The world was made by him, yet the world which continues to search for him beyond the skies or in otherworldly places will know him not in our age.

Can we not then open our eyes to life? Can it not be said that when we find the love that gives us the courage to be, to love, to share, to give, to care, to live, then we will have discovered God? God is not identified with these things, but he is revealed through them.

Is it too much to suggest that to know God in life is to experience transcendence, meaning, timelessness? If this is not foreign to our life, can "heaven" be so strange a word or concept? We have known in our personal histories what it means to have our life touched with the love and joy of fulfillment that transforms our history. Is this not the meaning of heaven?

When you and I are alive to this reality, then we can pray to the God who is in heaven, for heaven will stand for any and every moment in which eternity touches time with the gift of love. Heaven will be to live in what Paul Tillich calls the "eternal now."

"Our Father who art in heaven": Source of Life and Giver of all things, you are with us in our world. Help us to see, to know, and to be alive to your love so that we may live now and forever.

CHAPTER 4

The Call to Holiness

>>>>>>> W I L L I A M   S H A K E S P E A R E asked, "What's in a name?" and, answering his own question, immediately concluded:

> that which we call a rose
> By any other name would smell as sweet.
> —*Romeo and Juliet,* II, 2

Yet if any idea ever intrigued the Old Testament mind, it was the meaning of a name. The word "name" is used in the Old Testament some seven hundred and fifty times and in the book of Psalms, no less than ninety-eight. For the Hebrew there was mystery, power, and substance in a name. The biblical writers went to great pains to show the right order about naming. To name someone or something was to control it, to dominate it. God named Adam (Genesis 3:21); Adam named the animals (Genesis 2:20); and parents named their children (Genesis 4:1f.).

A name was also an insight into the character of a person. Hence when the character of the person changed, his name was changed also. So Abram, after being called to establish a new nation, became Abraham (Genesis 17:15). Jacob, after wrestling with the angel, became Israel (Genesis 3:28). Sometimes the message of the prophets was spoken through the naming of the child. Thus Isaiah speaking to Judah near the end of her history could name his son Shear Yashub, which meant "a remnant shall return" (Isaiah 7:3).

Perhaps the strangest note of the Old Testament in regard to names occurred in that the name of God could never be spoken by a faithful Hebrew. It was blasphemy to utter the holy name. When written in Hebrew, God's name was an unpronounceable set of consonants, YHWH. Biblically, to call one by name was to know the person, to be his equal, to have power over him. God to the Hebrew was mystery, depth beyond penetration. His fullness was unknowable, beyond comprehension. His name could not be spoken. The Ten Commandments enjoined the Jewish people not to take that holy name in vain (Exodus 20:7). When Jesus taught his disciples to pray, he asked them to say, "Hallowed be thy name" (Matthew 6:9). Hence in our worship for two thousand years we have repeated this phrase, "hallowed be thy name." It comes out of a rich Old Testament heritage. In this chapter we attempt to penetrate the meaning of the name of God, which name we pray in the Lord's Prayer to be ever hallowed.

The name of God is the key to the meaning of the story in Exodus of the call of Moses at the burning bush (Exodus 3:1–14; 4:31). Moses was summoned to be a leader, to be what he never dreamed of becoming. He was frightened. He argued, "Who am I to go to Pharaoh? They will not believe me. I am not an eloquent man." Finally, Moses said to the Lord of the burning bush, "They will want to know who sent me. What will I say? What, Lord, is your name?" And the Lord responded enigmatically, "I am what I am," or "I will be what I will be." Not much of an answer, it would seem. Yet perhaps it was that they could not grasp it then. Moses was busily reciting his shortcomings, his failures, his insecurities. God was saying, "You will know my name when you know who you are. To know God is to be who you are. I am the Source of Life," or as Paul Tillich might have translated, "My name is not something you say, it is something you are." Moses did not quite understand, yet that experience of God changed his life. He grasped his being, overcame his sense of inadequacy, and he became what he was capable of being. This man, beyond equal in the Old Testament, placed the stamp of his genius upon the Hebrew nation. In Moses the Hebrew nation found its birth, its destiny, its sense of identity. In meeting God Moses found himself, his power, and his being, but he never quite understood God's name.

Almost fourteen hundred years later another child of Abraham appeared in human history. He was a child of promise whose parents named him *Yeshua,* Joshua, or Jesus. It was a name which meant "deliverer" (Matthew 1:21). It was to be his destiny to make the name of God known to all the world. This Jesus said rather astounding things: "The Father and I are one" (John 10:30). "He who has seen me has seen the Father" (John 14:19). "No man comes to the Father but by me" (John 14:16). "I have come that you might have life" (John 10:10). It was said of him on the first Palm Sunday, "Blessed is he that comes in the name of the Lord" (Luke 19:38). And after the events of Easter, people were baptized "in the name of Jesus" (Acts 2:38). They were asked to believe "in his name" (1 John 3:23).

The name of Jesus became synonymous with the name of God. How so? Because Jesus revealed the nature of God as the Ground of Being, the Source of Love. He revealed it not by talking about it, but by living it, by being what he was. God's name is not something you say, it is something you are. Jesus was open to his world, alive, free, and whole. It could be said of Jesus, "I am who I am." He reflected the gifts of life, of being, of love. Men who followed him found themselves called into their own life, their destiny to be themselves. So deeply did Jesus possess his life that he was free to give his life away, loving even his tormentors; people saw in him the Source of Life itself, a Source which death could not destroy. God is the Ground of Being. He is the Source of Love. He is the Depth of Life. Jesus has revealed what life in touch with that God can be: open, free, whole, selfless; and Paul could write: "If any man is in Christ Jesus, he is a new creature" (2 Corinthians 5:17).

This is why Paul also could suggest that "at the name of Jesus every knee shall bow" (Philippians 2:10). It is the bow of gratitude. It is the acknowledgment that before we can be ourselves, life has to be given to us; before we can love, we have to be loved. This human truth so familiar to contemporary psychiatrists is the reality that lies behind the biblical word "grace." Christ *is* the Giver. Grace and truth come through Jesus Christ (John 1:17). His name stands for his being, the power of his life. Lives touched by his life are set free to be. We bow at the mention of his name to acknowledge the Source of our own life. We Christians are receivers who are compelled to give. We are dependent on the Source of our life, but we express that dependence with the maturity of caring and outgoing love. To symbolize this we are named in baptism: signed with his cross and sealed by his name.

In the power of his love we are capable of loving. In the power of his affirmation we are free to be ourselves without apology or boasting and, wonder of wonders, we are free to let others be themselves without our feeling threatened by either their success or failure. In the power of forgiveness we can forgive ourselves and discover the grace to accept the weaknesses of another without the self-serving rejection of judgment. It is in the being and doing of these things that we hallow the name of the God who has called us into life.

We still cannot fathom the depths of the God who is the Source of Life. We cannot fully say his name or exhaust his meaning. However, we can know his power and share his love. As we do so, we make his name holy. This is what we mean when we pray, "Hallowed be thy name."

CHAPTER 5

God's Kingdom

>>>->>> O N E   O F the most fascinating aspects of scholarship to me is the study of the development of a word, especially some frequently used word in the vocabulary of theology. In this chapter I want to examine the word "kingdom," especially as it relates to that phrase in the Lord's Prayer where we are taught to pray, "Thy kingdom come."

The word "kingdom" first appears in the biblical tradition simply as the name of a political entity, the kingdom of Edom or Moab, for example (Numbers 24:7). It was considered by the Hebrews to be an evil thing (1

Samuel 8:11ff.). A kingdom had a king who enslaved, taxed, and conscripted his people. The Hebrews were cautious about kings; they never made Moses or Joshua their king. At the beginning of their national history, their ideal was local self-government in loose confederation. In fact, during the period of the Judges, they practiced a kind of states rights, resisting all attempts at the centralization of power.

However, the forces of history, including the need for self-preservation, finally compelled the people of Israel to ask for a king. "Give us a king that we might be like other nations," they petitioned the prophet and judge, Samuel (1 Samuel 8:5). He, loyal to the loose-confederation period of Hebrew history, was slow to move. He saw a king as a threat to his leadership. When he finally did respond to the pressure for a monarch, his latent fear of strong, centralized government caused Samuel to establish a very limited monarchy over which he would continue to have authority. This limitation of power was a factor in preventing Saul, the first king, from establishing a dynasty.

Certainly if the biblical record is historically accurate, it did not help Saul's cause when Samuel anointed David as his successor while Saul was still living. In any event, after Saul the royal house of David came to power and ruled for many generations, achieving its period of most material splendor during the reign of Solomon, David's son. With Solomon the word kingdom began for the first time to have religious connotations, particularly after the military defeat, the long exile, and finally the return of the Hebrews in the fourth century to their homeland. For this is the period when they idealized the kingdom of Solomon, yearned for the splendor of his reign, and incorporated these yearnings in the patterns of their worship (1 Chronicles 29:11). Israel is referred to as the kingdom of the Lord (1 Chronicles 28:5). Homage paid the king began to color the form in which homage was paid to God in worship. The king was the epitome of power, status, and influence. He was the pinnacle of human success, and his kingship became the primary analogy by which men understood God. The Hebrews began to picture God on a throne. They spoke to him only on bended knee, they extolled his virtues, they sang his praises, and his domain they called the "kingdom of heaven." Our religious language has not yet escaped the influence of this attitude.

To the Hebrews the kingdom of God was the description of earthly kingdoms perfected. God's kingdom would be everlasting, not brief (Psalm 145:13). It would possess glory and splendor, not instability and problems (Psalm 145:11).

When this tiny nation of Hebrews was buffeted or defeated in the tides of world history, more and more did its people hope for that kingdom which could not be buffeted or defeated. The more the Hebrews were stripped of all vestiges of human power, splendor, and prestige, the more they began to pray that "the kingdom" would come and the more vivid became their image of that kingdom. The One who would usher in that kingdom they called Messiah, and in him they placed their hope for future fulfillment.

The Messiah would be the answer to their needs. Since they were weak, he would be strong, a mighty conqueror, a kingly man, a fitting and worthy son of David. He would inaugurate the kingdom of God in which they would share. Messiah was the embodiment of their human yearning. He would overcome their discontent. It was under the symbols of "kingdom of God" and "Messiah" that the Hebrews expressed their lack of fulfillment and revealed the hope of glory which they did not possess. They were grasping at a life bigger than they were living, and a meaning greater than they had found.

Within this context and against this background, a first-century Jewish man broke upon the stage of history announcing that "the kingdom of heaven is at hand" (Mark 1:15). Yet in no detail did he fulfill the expected image. This man, a son of David? Hardly! (Matthew 12:23) His mother was a peasant girl, and his father a carpenter. He hailed from Nazareth, a second-rate village. This man a kingly figure? Why he owned nothing! He had been born in a stable and his associates were tax collectors, publicans, prostitutes, fishermen. This man on a throne in Jerusalem? Why, he was executed in a public place, buried in a borrowed tomb!

Yet this man looked beneath the imagery surrounding "kingdom" and "Messiah" and discovered what the deepest human yearnings expressed in these words really were. Then to these yearnings he spoke. He took this word "kingdom" and made it the center of his message (Mark 1:14), announced that in and through his life it was at hand, told what was required to enter it, and urged his disciples to pray, "Thy kingdom come" (Matthew 6:10).

We will continue to pray this prayer, I submit, only when we can discover what this word meant to our Christ.

To Jesus of Nazareth God's kingdom is not a realm over which God rules, but it is a quality of life in which God is seen; it is a presence, a life-giving power. The kingdom of which Jesus spoke is seen not in the splendor of wealth, but rather in gifts of wholeness and healing. The kingdom is revealed not in the mighty, he said, but in the poor in spirit (Matthew 5:3). Those who, when persecuted for the sake of righteousness, do not sink into bitterness and despair are the revealers of the kingdom (Matthew 5:10). Kingdom is the quality of openness to the stranger, the poor, the little children, the broken, the judged.* The kingdom is that presence, that quality, that joy of life before which the value of everything else pales by comparison. So it is the pearl of great price (Matthew 13:46). It is the insignificant mustard seed that grows into dominance (13:18f.). It is the leaven that gives worth and quality to the whole loaf (13:33). The kingdom is seen in the gift of humility which is not an

---

* See Luke 13:29; Matthew 19:23; 18:4; 22:1f.; 7:21.

attitude of self-deprecation, but the ability to be and to accept what one is. The kingdom is seen when, in a state of tiptoe expectancy, we look for fulfillment that we are certain is coming, for we have tasted it already (Matthew 25:1ff.). This is the kingdom which Jesus proclaims, the kingdom he inaugurates. He brings it because he brings love; and when love touches life, it reveals to us the joy and the peace that are the marks of the kingdom.

We are thus invited into the kingdom, but we are also told to pray for its coming. We rejoice in its presence, yet long for its completion. We see it wherever love is shared, life is lived, freedom is experienced, and fear is overcome. But it is always but a glimpse, a fleeting moment. When we meet God in the joy of human community, we become immediately aware that we cannot encompass him. He is the "beyond in our midst," but always the "beyond." We meet him in life and love only to know that he is infinite, transcendent Life and Love.

When we respond to this presence of God in life, we discover dimensions of life never before even within our reach. We become persons we never before imagined ourselves capable of being, but we also know that there is ever so much more we want to be.

Every taste of fulfillment simply broadcasts the desire for total fulfillment. Every mount of transfiguration simply emphasizes the parts of life which are not transfigured. So it is that even as we rejoice in the dawning of the kingdom, we pray that the kingdom will come and we acknowledge that it is not yet here.

It was Augustine, the fifth-century theologian, who observed in his *Confessions:* "Thou, Oh God, hast made us for thyself alone, and our hearts are restless until they find their rest in thee." Restlessness is awakened by the experience of life and love announcing the presence of the kingdom of God. Restlessness is sustained by the incomplete hold on life and love that marks every child of God who is a citizen of that kingdom. To pray "Thy kingdom come" is to acknowledge and accept the reality of incompleteness as part of the Christian life. It is to live in the joy of discontent. I know of no place in the Bible where the Christ promises contentment or peace of mind. He promises the "peace which passeth understanding," which to me is the peace that surpasses understanding and enables us to live in the midst of tension and conflict and the lack of fulfillment. I see him pronouncing his blessing on those who hunger and on those who thirst. They are the ones who refuse to allow any god substitute to rob them of the humanity which they celebrate and experience when they are touched by the kingdom.

The kingdom of God does not create peace, contentment, and satisfaction. Instead it brings to life an ultimate affirmation and love that is so deep that we can live in the midst of human discontent without despairing, that we can face the broken and unfulfilled quality of life without depression or inertia. To be in the kingdom is to rejoice in who we are, the loved children of God, while we still yearn for what we shall be. It is being able to envision the world perfected while we live in the world that is. It is refusing either to be content with what is or overpowered to inertia by what is not yet. The victory is won, but the battle must continue to rage.

The kingdom has come. It is within us whenever the love of God stands us on our feet and calls us to be the self we are. There is security, but not perfection, in this. The kingdom will come. It will arrive when all that shall be *is*. We live in the joy of discontent, full citizens of the realm that is yet to be.

"Thy kingdom come." To pray for it is to rejoice in it, even as we work for it and yearn for it.

CHAPTER 6

God's Will
—Our Will

➤➤➤-➤➤➤ PERHAPS no other words flow so freely from the lips of well-intentioned people as the phrase "the will of God." God is blamed for so much!

This phrase, "the will of God," harbors much ambiguity. What is the will of God? Can we recognize it, identify it, be sure of it? Can we separate it from *our* desires, *our* vested interests? Does the will of God happen? Has it happened? Can we make it happen? What does it mean?

I remember well my first experience of death in the ministry. I had been in that town only about two weeks

when a call came informing me that a man, the father
of two boys, ages fourteen and nine, had died. To
heighten the tragedy, I learned that this man and his
wife had separated about three weeks previously and
she had moved away, leaving the boys with their father.
The boys had thus suffered the trauma of losing their
mother by separation and their father by death in the
space of less than a month. No other relatives lived in
the area.

When I arrived at the family home, the resources of
the community were already being gathered. I first met
the elder son, who was wearing the mask of manly com-
posure. Then I went back to the bedroom to meet
Johnny, the nine-year-old. He was in the clutches of a
well-meaning, devout Christian lady who was doing her
best to bring comfort. Tears were streaming down Johnny's fat cheeks. I entered just in time to hear the lady
tell Johnny that God wanted his daddy to come to
heaven to be with him, that his death was God's will.
To that statement Johnny looked up and replied, "Well,
damn God!" The lady was horrified. For all I know, she
has not stopped shaking yet. She looked as though she
expected a lightning bolt to strike both of them dead.

I thought about Johnny's response for a long time
after that. Any god who is so incomplete that he needs
to rob little boys of their fathers is a demon who deserves
the condemnation which Johnny so brazenly spoke. I
think it is the best response I have ever heard to the
confused statements of people who equate whatever

happens with the will of God, as if his will were passive toward the event and a pat explanation for anything that might happen.

But what do we mean when we pray, "Thy will be done"? Can we repeat these words with meaning? What is the will of the biblical God whom we meet in life, and what does it mean to pray for his will to be done? These are the questions for us to answer.

Strangely enough, reference to the will of God is almost nonexistent in the Old Testament. Among the Hebrew people, the Law was considered to be the revealed will of God; hence reference was always to the Law, seldom to God's will. Even when the psalmist cried "Teach me thy will, O Lord" (Psalm 143:10), he really meant "teach me thy Law," which the Jewish mind identified with the Torah.

In the New Testament, the phrase "the will of God" is used sparingly. When Paul uses the phrase, he almost always means "destiny" by it. He refers to himself as destined to be an apostle "by the will of God" (1 Corinthians 1:1), or he speaks of visiting a particular church "if it be God's will" (Romans 1:10). When we investigate the gospels, we find that only Matthew and John use the phrase "the will of God" with any regularity. Even more unusual is the realization that the Lord's Prayer is given us only in Matthew and Luke, and Luke's version specifically omits the clause "thy will be done on earth as it is in heaven" (Luke 11:2f.). Only Matthew records these words in the Lord's Prayer (Matthew 6:10).

So in order to find the meaning of this phrase, I believe we have to analyze its meaning to Matthew, the author of the first Gospel.

To Matthew "the will of God" is always an active phrase. The one who does the will of God is like a tree bearing good fruit. The fruit of your life—love, joy, peace—announces the obedience, or lack of it, to the will of God. On one occasion in Matthew's story, Jesus' mother and his brothers, somewhat embarrassed at the public spectacle of his ministry, come to take him away. Jesus declines to go and disclaims the tie of his own family by announcing, "Who is my mother and who are my brothers? The ones who do the will of God are my kinsmen" (Matthew 12:46). It is not in verbal declarations, but in the active doing of God's will that Matthew places Jesus' emphasis. The same note is struck in a parable which only Matthew records. It is the story of two brothers. To one the father said, "Son, go work in the vineyard today," to which the son answered, "I will not." But afterward he was sorry about this response, and so he went and worked faithfully. To the second son the father made the same request. The second son answered immediately, "I go, sir." But he did not go. Which, Jesus asks, did the will of the father? (Matthew 21:28) Again and again Matthew drives home Jesus' point: The will of God is seen in what we do, rather than in what we say.

Finally, the phrase "the will of God" is the key to the episode of Jesus in the Garden of Gethsemane. When

the moment of crucifixion is unavoidably near, Jesus
prays, "Not my will but thine be done" (Matthew
26:29ff.). "If this cup cannot pass unless I drink it, thy
will be done." Jesus saw his life and his death as a
deliberate living-out of the will of God. It was a life of
giving, loving, and caring. It was a life in which his
words found expression in his deeds, and his deeds were
the acting out of his words. It was a life that possessed
the courage to be what he was, whether responding to
popularity or persecution. To do the will of God was to
call people to life, the life which he possessed in abun-
dance.

His life was the one life in which God fulfilled his
purpose of love. It was the power of love that healed
the sick. It was the power of love that reconciled the
estranged, that reached out to the stranger. It was the
power of love that raised the dead and called men to
life. It was the power of love that gave peace and joy and
united the scattered children into one body. Perfect love
in action reveals the will of God. It was this life, this
man who lived this way, who taught us to pray, "Thy
will be done on earth as it is in heaven." It is also this
man who gives us the marching orders: "As my Father
has sent me to do this work of love, so send I you" (John
20:21).

To do the will of God in our time, to put perfect love
into action, this is our task. To pray, "Thy will be
done," and then to do nothing is to broadcast hypocrisy.
It is to allow our words and our lives to be in visible dis-

agreement. It is to sacrifice our authenticity. It is to live a lie.

The will of God is life, wholeness, love for all of his children. Can these words be anything but a cruel joke to those who live in the despair of poverty? If this world has the ability to feed its population, yet people die of starvation, can God's will be done? If people go to bed hungry and malnourished in the cities of this affluent land, can we still pray the Lord's Prayer?

The will of God is love for all of his children. Can love be real where discrimination continues to exist? If the color of my skin bars me from any privilege, any neighborhood, or any activity another man may have, can love be true? So long as discrimination and prejudice exist in our world, in our lives, can we continue to pray the Lord's Prayer, "Thy will be done"? Are we not in danger of being like the brother in the parable who says with his lips, "Yes, I'll go and work in the vineyard," and yet he never goes? God's work is here to be done. When will we do it?

God's will is also for peace and life, not war and death. Yet the history of our world is a history of warfare as the means of settling disputes. Great world struggles and limited but frightfully brutal wars dot the pages of our recent history: Korea, Vietnam, Ireland, the Middle East, Pakistan. In the name of civilization, or of stopping communism, or of preserving democracy, or of a thousand other noble ideals, we seem willing to watch people decimated, land defoliated, and spirits crushed when idealism is a casualty of battle. Can Christians pray, "Thy will be done," and not rise to full responsibility in the human struggle to see that wars cease throughout the world?

Over and over again Jesus' point is that our deeds must match our words if this prayer is to be real. We cannot pray, "Thy will be done," unless we are willing to act, to exercise our power to bring life, forgiveness, healing, and transfiguration to our world. "Thy will be done" means that we, too, must reproduce the miracle of the loaves and fish in order that we might feed the hungry. "Thy will be done" means that we must bring life where death reigns supreme, hope where despair is overwhelming, peace where hatred, fear, suspicion, discrimination, and war abound. For the fullness of life— love, joy, and peace—is the will of God, says Jesus. To pray for it is to be willing to work for it—to live it. If we are not willing to live it, then let our lips be mute and our tongues be silent whenever we kneel to pray.

CHAPTER 7

His Gift of Daily Bread

⇶⇶ I N T H E Bible bread seems to touch every aspect of life and to be associated with innumerable themes. Bread fascinated the biblical writers, and they used the word literally and symbolically more than three hundred times.

Bread is first mentioned in the Genesis story when God meted out punishment to the disobedient Adam and Eve. "You shall eat bread," he said, "until you return to the ground" (Genesis 3:19). The eating of bread, which could be made only by man's hard labor, was a part of the punishment. But bread in the biblical story quickly came to be a synonym for all food, the staff of life. The Hebrew people felt themselves miraculously delivered from starvation after their escape from Egypt when they discovered bread in the wilderness, which they called manna from heaven (Exodus 16:4ff.). Something so essential to life inevitably finds its way into men's worship; hence it is not surprising to discover in the early Jewish temple the shewbread of the Presence, the bread which was the sign of the love and favor of God.

In the account of the temptation of Jesus, the tempter suggested to Jesus that the Messianic sign was the ability to turn stones into bread. But Jesus responded, "Man does not live by bread alone" (Matthew 4:3–4). Yet later in referring to his teaching, Jesus said, "It is not fair to take the children's bread and throw it to the dogs" (Matthew 15:26). In John's Gospel Jesus referred to himself as the Bread of Life, the New Manna, if you will (John 6:41). On the night in which he was betrayed, he took bread, broke it, and identified it with his body (Luke 22:19). Finally, the gospels tell us that the risen Lord made himself known to his disciples "in the breaking of bread" (Luke 24:35). It is very natural, then, that when our Lord taught us to pray, he included in that prayer a bread petition, "Give us this day our daily bread" (Matthew 6:11). Bread has, therefore, become an essential element in Christian prayer and worship.

These words almost always are interpreted as the prayer of a hungry child before an all-powerful Father.

Perhaps that is inevitable, given the ancient struggle for survival that marked the lives of our forefathers. For ancient men had to wrest their living from the earth one day at a time. Food was not easily stored or preserved in that period. Hunger was an ever-present reality, starvation an ever-fearful threat. Our ancestors were at the mercy of the sun, the soil, and the rain, forces which they could not control and before which they stood in worshipful awe. To them the power that directed these forces was the Source of Life. This power they called God. To him they looked for favor and for help, while on him they felt quite dependent. Their dependency had a childlike quality to it. Before God, they were hungry children, empty bowl in hand, asking for daily bread. It is in this context that we tend to hear this petition in the Lord's Prayer.

The comparatively affluent Western man of the scientific twentieth century, however, finds this concept foreign to his experience. The starving masses on the Indian subcontinent may find it relevant, but the urban technocrat of America certainly does not. This modern man or woman is not mystified by natural forces. He understands crop rotation and soil erosion. He employs chemical fertilizers, scientific breeding procedures, and irrigation. In highly developed nations his production rate is so superior that governments pay him not to plant all his acreage, but instead to invest it in soil banks, if you will. This modern man is not humble before his accomplishments. In many parts of the world, he has conquered the ancient enemy of hunger. He is not a child begging for food with an empty bowl in hand. If "give us this day our daily bread" presents this image to him, he finds difficulty saying this prayer because he cannot in truth relate to the actual fear of hunger. He has never known hunger.

How often it is that we interpret the words of our faith in terms of the ancient world alone, force the world view of yesterday into their meaning, and thereby make them nonsensical for the man of today! How often have we Christians presented this modern world with a picture of God that literally violates the dignity and creative power of man; a God whose greatest delight comes in having men reduce themselves to children and beg before him, plead with him or beseech him for a favor, and always, mind you, from the humiliating position of a slave on bended knee before a master! Perhaps the modern revolt against organized religion is rooted at least in part in a rediscovery of human dignity and the call of man to be man, full and mature and not a powerless child before an omnipotent father. If this be so, then perhaps contemporary atheism has within it some profoundly Christian elements, if only we could embrace what it is saying.

Can we strip away this image of God? Can we, in the full dignity and creativity of the modern spirit, confront the words of the Lord's Prayer, "Give us this day our daily bread," and hear these words with meaning in our generation? If we insist that God in some mysterious and capricious manner is the One who gives bread to his children, then the hungry masses in the underdeveloped countries of the world must believe him to be quite demonic. This feeling is so beautifully and honestly illustrated by the fact that ancient Mayans in Guatemala destroyed the faces of their idols when their crops were bad. If God is the One who gives human beings their daily bread, then he is a very inadequate and very impotent God to the two out of every three persons in this world who go to bed hungry every night. If somehow we expect God, quite apart from men, to do the necessary work of feeding the hungry, then God will be a dying myth, clung to until the last, only by those whose stomachs are full.

It is a strange experience to sit before a magnificent banquet table and hear the master of the house give thanks for the food and piously beseech God "to provide for the needs of others," as if we expect him to rain down bread on the starving masses of the world. That is the prayer of irresponsibility and such irresponsibility is the mark of a child, not a man; it is the mark of a child who is dependent, incapable of acting, unwilling to assume the stance of maturity.

Does God have any other way to provide for the needs of men except through the responsible actions of men: better production rates, better methods of sharing both food and agricultural know-how, cessation of the exploitation of inadequate prices paid for the produce of the underprivileged of our world, and sensible population control? What can be said about us when we use the fruits of our labor, our technology, and our creativity simply to stuff ourselves while we piously petition God to provide for the needs of others? What do we mean, then, when we Christians of the twentieth century pray, "Give us this day our daily bread"?

First, let us state categorically that the man Jesus, who taught us to pray this prayer, was anything but an infantile man, childlike or irresponsible. The One who claimed to have a special and unique relationship with God lived his life out in total freedom and full power, possessing his being with courage and dignity. It was his stated purpose to call men into being, to set men free, to give life and to give it abundantly (John 8:36; 10:10). The God Jesus proclaimed was a God who was constantly giving to men. God's gift, however, was never a daily handout of the strong to the weak, nor was it an allowance that a parent might pay to a child. God's great gift was, and is, the gift of love which calls us into being, into freedom, into independence, and full maturity so that man might claim the dignity of being the image of God by acting like a creator, by being a giver and not only a receiver, by being a source of life to his world, not a leech upon his world. It was the man who revealed this concept of God, who taught us to pray, "Give us our daily bread."

To say this prayer is to acknowledge that we are the recipients of bread, of life. It is to recognize that the Source of Bread is the Source of Life and that as he has shared his life, his bread, with us to bring us into creative, responsible maturity, so now we must share our life, our bread, with his creation. In no other way can we express the image of God.

"I am the bread of life" (John 6:48). "This bread is my body, broken for you" (Luke 22:19). If we feed on that bread, if we participate in that life, then we must wake up to love, and live and share now just as he did. This means we cannot pray for daily bread unless we are willing to assume responsibility for every man created in his image who hungers in body or in spirit for life.

To pray for our daily bread is to acknowledge that we are men and women—full, creative, mature men and women—capable of accepting the responsibility for our world, willing to be our brothers' keepers. "Give us daily bread" is thus first a prayer of thanksgiving that we have been the recipients of the bread of life, and secondly, it is our commitment to share that gift with all the world. If we cannot be giving, responsible, loving people sharing our gift of life, then we make a mockery of our prayer for daily bread.

CHAPTER 8

Forgiveness and Wholeness

⇥⇥⇥⇥ H A R R Y A N G S T R O M , the star of John Updike's novel *Rabbit Run*, observed, "As a human being I'm a C-." Most of us, like Harry Angstrom, hope that judgment, whether divine or human, will be on a wide curve.

If I had to name the one central and all-important ingredient in life, it would be forgiveness. Without forgiveness no friendship could ever be sustained, no marriage could ever be successful, no partnership could ever last. Forgiveness is that quality of life which is necessary to every person who wants to escape loneliness, isolation, fear. It is the very matrix of community, the meaning of any relationship.

Yet strangely enough, the word "forgiveness" is not a word that occurs frequently in the biblical story. It is found in the Old Testament more often than in the New Testament. Only once does the Gospel of John employ the word (John 20:23). Paul uses it only four times.* When it occurs in the Old Testament, the word "forgiveness" is almost always used in a legal sense. It means to wipe clean the slate, to overlook a debt, to refuse to enact the punishment.† Because the New Testament tends to express in different words its understanding of forgiveness, it is almost inevitable that we tend to hear the word "forgive" in the Old Testament legalistic, moralistic sense.

This understanding is reinforced by our somewhat unfortunate translation of the Lord's Prayer. The petition, "Forgive us our trespasses, as we forgive those who trespass against us" (Luke 11:14), has an almost legalistic ring to it. It sounds as if we are making a deal: "God we forgive so that you will forgive." We seem to assume that God is an authority bent upon punishing us as delinquent children. So we approach him with a bargain and the offer of our good example: "Lord forgive us as we have forgiven others." We have only to state the matter in this way to see the violence we do to the very idea of God. We make him a petty sovereign created in

* 2 Corinthians 2:7, 2:10, 12:13; Colossians 3:13.
† Genesis 50:17; Numbers 30:8; 1 Kings 8:34; Psalm 32:5.

the image of man, seeking to satisfy a human scale of justice. Such an understanding of God causes many to dismiss the whole Christian story as unbelievable.

But if we desire to understand forgiveness as Jesus understood and exemplified it in his life, then we must begin to rethink almost totally our idea of God. We must stop thinking of God after the analogy of man and stop reading into him the qualities we desire for ourselves and let God be God.

God is not a superperson who expresses human emotions. God does not get angry. The God of the Christian faith does not mete out rewards and punishments. The God revealed in Jesus Christ is the Power of Love (1 John 4:8). He is the Meaning of Life. It is you and I, human beings, who punish ourselves because of our fear, loneliness, and insecurity. We punish ourselves because we cut ourselves off from that which we most desperately need in order to live, namely the capacity to receive love and to give it, the capacity to receive forgiveness and to share it.

Yes God judges, but God's judgment is never the passing of a sentence, the execution of a punishment. It is, instead, a confrontation in which love reveals the distortion of our "unlove," and we have to see ourselves as we are. It is a confrontation in which life reveals our inability to live, and we have to see our unused potential. It is a confrontation in which forgiveness reveals the depth of our inadequacy, our guilt, and we have to admit our failure. This is the meaning of judgment.

If we cannot love another as he is, the reason is not that we are bad, but rather that we are cut off from the Source of Love. If we cannot forgive one who is different or threatening, it is because we have not experienced forgiveness deeply enough to face the threat of difference. If we are so busy trying to prove how important we are, it is not because we think too much of ourselves, but because we think too little and because we are not securely grounded in the Source of Life. It is when we are unable to be what we are that we cannot allow others to be what they are. We thus become judges of relative human worth, snobs, and status-seekers revealing our separation from the God of love. God is not an avenging, punishing, wrathful deity, withholding his love and forgiveness. God *is* Love and Forgiveness. It is our fear, our loneliness, our separation that keep us apart from God and from each other. Unless this can be overcome, there will never be the relationship of community. At this level we begin to understand the real meaning of forgiveness.

It was a startling experience for me to discover that everyone is insecure, that I was not alone in this. Because none of us has ever viewed life through anyone else's emotional eyes, we sometimes think that in human relationships we are the only scared party. But once our eyes are opened to the need for forgiveness in every person, we begin to see how life is organized with forgiveness and acceptance built in to create the supportive structure we need in order to feel secure.

The city of New York seems frantic and frightening to many a non-New Yorker. It appears cold, distant, unfriendly. A stranger never sees a familiar face, and he thinks that everyone else must be having a similar experience. Several years ago I had to be in New York for about ten days. Across the street from my hotel was a quick-order coffee shop. The food was terrible, but the convenience was such that I ate breakfast there each morning. The first morning everyone seemed strange, and I assumed that they were all unknown to each other as well as to me. But several days went by and I became aware of the fact that these people returned to this coffee shop daily, occupied the same seats, and in many instances ate the same food. Indeed the waitress did not wait for some of them to order. She placed their breakfast before them without a word passing between them. In that coffee shop they belonged, they were known, they were even important. They had created a community of support that enabled them to function in a giant city. In the quiet acceptance of their belonging they were experiencing forgiveness. When I realized that they were not the threats to my security so much as I was the threat to theirs, I became sensitive and communicated "forgiveness" to them. Out of this developed many memorable conversations. We were all looking for love, for warmth, for security. When we understood this and forgave the threat and fear we created in each other, we could and did meet.

In one of my former congregations there was a man

who was at the very top of the community's social ladder. He had wealth, power, prestige; in fact, he had everything a man could need to be secure, I thought. People deferred to him on all sides. When he spoke in a social gathering everyone listened. When he told a joke, even a bad joke, everyone laughed. He was a commanding and, to this young clergyman, a frightening figure. He seemed so important that I hated to impose upon him. How badly I misjudged him! He became ill while I was his minister, and I went dutifully to see him. His guard was down as it tends to be in sickness, and he revealed to me a desperately lonely man. He never knew whether or not people were honest with him, whether he was liked or feared. He thought everyone was out to use him for their own purposes. The only way he could live with these feelings was to stay in control of every situation at all times. He kept a book by his bed in which were inscribed the names of those who called on him in his sickness—a rather desperate attempt at ego-building. His public image of being the social lion was the way he ministered to his insecurities. When he showed me who he was, he was confessing and revealing his inner being to me. When I responded by accepting his revelation, I was forgiving. Then I was able to show him who I was, to confess my fear, and he, in turn, was able to respond by hearing and understanding—that was forgiveness. Our mutual insecurities no longer kept us locked in fear inside ourselves. Confession was followed by forgiveness, which created community. How important it is to see that neither sin nor forgiveness can be understood on a moralistic level! Deeds are but expressions of our being.

The Bible asserts that we are born in sin, that "in sin hath my mother conceived me" (Psalm 51:5). The biblical story assumes that sin is universal or original, but when it does assume this, it is not referring to bad deeds that we, our parents, or our ancestors ever committed. It is, rather, describing human nature living in the absence of perfect love, manifesting the human characteristics of self-rejection, self-judgment, inadequacy, insecurity, and fear. We are separated from one another and afraid of one another, not because we are bad, but because the love in our life is inadequate. Sin is a description of the brokenness, the insecurity of our being from whence arises the destructive, self-centered behavior of our life.

Examine the moral misdeeds of our society—murder, adultery, gossip, lying, stealing, prejudice, exploitation, and so on for as long a list as you wish to make. Follow each of these actions to its roots and see if it is not a manifestation of the person's need to recompense himself for an inadequacy that he feels deeply. Such needs are in every one of us. This is the root meaning of sin in the Bible. It is a description of our *being*, not our doing. It is the lack of love that cripples, breaks and distorts us, the insecurity that separates us from each other in fear, the self-negativity that we project outward. It is to this level of life that forgiveness must speak if it is to be real.

Forgiveness is the healing of our broken lives. It is the acceptance of ourselves as we are. It is the affirmation of our being that enables us to venture outside our shells and live. Since God is the Source of Life and the Source of Love, forgiveness is the experience of God which gives us our very life, our ability to love, to accept, and to live. Forgiveness is also the experience of redemption, the overcoming of sin. Since love and life were perfectly revealed in Jesus our Christ, we can and do say of him that he has overcome the sin of the world.

People hear this proclamation and they become disturbed because no emphasis is placed on the necessity to struggle individually with our weaknesses. For many this opens the door to permissiveness, fatalism, inertia, or other frightening fears. But the only way any of us can deal effectively with our inadequacies is to receive from another a deeper sense of our being. We stop gossiping when we no longer need to build ourselves up by tearing another down. We stop lying when we can face the truth about ourselves in honesty and do not need to create an ego-satisfying dream world of unreality. We no longer have an emotional need to be prejudiced when the freedom of our own self-acceptance is expressed in our ability to accept another as he is. Any struggle for self-improvement finally must be on the level of being rather than on the level of doing. No insight seems more difficult than this for many to grasp.

In the parable of the Last Judgment, the King separates the sheep from the goats. The goats he assigns to hell with these words: "When I was hungry you gave me no food, naked and ye clothed me not; I was imprisoned and you did not visit me, thirsty and you gave me no drink" (Matthew 25:32ff.). The condemned are astonished at this judgment. "Lord we never saw you and failed to minister to you." And the Lord of the Judgment acknowledges, "How right you are. You did not minister to me because you never were able to see me. You could not see me because you did not love me."

Is this not always true of human relationships? When I was a child learning the ways of my prejudiced society, I recall hearing an older man explain his difficulty in remembering the features of any black man. When he met one, he saw only the blackness, not the person. He never realized that his problem was a deficiency of his caring, not of his seeing.

It was, then, rather refreshing later to meet this phenomenon in reverse. In a city where I formerly lived, a sister church called a new minister who had spent his entire previous ministry in the Orient. After three weeks in this southern city he astounded his congregation by confessing his difficulty in learning the names of the children in the Sunday School. "All these little Anglo-Saxon children look alike to me," he admitted. His hearers grimaced to find themselves victims of the same blindness that they had unknowingly been guilty of all along. When we do not love we cannot see. If we do not love, we will never recognize another's need. The sin of our life will blind us. Forgiveness is that power that accepts, affirms, and frees us to be sensitive and open to the potential for life in every relationship. Forgiveness touches our *being*.

Look at the marriages that fail because each partner is so tied up in his own fears that he can neither see nor love his mate. Look at the generation gap, the racial divisions, the barriers between rich and poor. We cannot understand each other, we cannot see each other, because we do not love each other. Our isolation causes us to be aware only of the threat or fear another poses. We feel our status and our values are on trial. Unless love and forgiveness free us to be what we are, we cannot reach out to the young or the old, the rich or the poor, the black or the white, husband or wife, and build a relationship, a sense of community.

Love and forgiveness, then, enable us to see each other as we are, to call each other into being. This is the meaning of forgiveness in the New Testament. It is a synonym for love. God, the Source of Love and Life, ever seeks to break through our barriers to love us, to call us into life. When we are open to him, we experience the power that enables us to risk ourselves, to give ourselves to each other in respect, love, and joy. When we are open to this love, we are lifted out of the insecurity of our isolation, enabled to make friends with our brothers, to see them, to understand them, to love them as they are.

When our lives reveal this quality of forgiveness, then we know what Jesus meant in the Lord's Prayer. "Forgive us our trespasses as we forgive those who trespass against us" is not a petition to a judge on a throne to effect a just bargain. It is a statement of fact about life when touched by the reality of God. The accepted life will accept; the forgiven life will forgive. The more deeply one accepts, forgives, and loves another, the more one will reveal the acceptance, love, and forgiveness of God which has set him free.

CHAPTER 9

When We Are Tested

➤➤➤➤➤➤ H U M A N emotions are interesting to observe and to study. They defy rational explanations and reveal hidden attitudes. Certainly this is the case among church people who are caught up in and buffeted by the winds of change that are sweeping through our century. The replacement in worship, for example, of the familiar with the new or strange usually creates an emotional, not a rational, response. When the music of worship is given a modern accent the security of many is upset. The more familiar the worship experience, the more emotional is the response to its change. Hence a

new communion service disturbs more people than a
new baptism or marriage service. Moreover, in various
traditions a new rendition of the creed has been particularly difficult for some. But the sharpest emotional
reaction seems to come when the congregation is invited
to pray "as our Saviour Christ taught us to pray," and
these unfamiliar phrases are heard:

> Our Father in heaven,
>   holy be your Name,
>   your kingdom come,
>   your will be done,
>   on earth as in heaven.
> Give us today our daily bread.
> Forgive us our sins
>   as we forgive those who sin against us.
> Do not bring us to the test
>   but deliver us from evil.
> For the kingdom, the power,
>   and the glory are yours
>   now and for ever. Amen.
>   —*Services for Trial Use, 1971*

In our surprise and anguish at a "new" Lord's Prayer,
we hear people remarking that "they" have even changed
the Lord's Prayer, "they" being those terrible people
somewhere who delight in making changes. One little
girl even asked if this meant that "they were recalling
the Lord's Prayer." Our words indicate that we believe
the familiar form of the Lord's Prayer is the original

version, the words of Jesus himself. We forget that in the sixteenth century when this familiar version of the Lord's Prayer was translated into English, its Elizabethan sound was the vernacular of that time. We forget that in the sixteenth century the Lord's Prayer was translated from Latin, from whence it had been translated from Greek, from whence it had been translated from the original Aramaic. Such an emotional response fails to comprehend the reality that language changes, words shift their meaning, and often if we refuse to change a word or a phrase, it means we are being unfaithful to the original intention of the prayer. Sometimes to refuse to change a phrase is to invite deliberate distortion, misunderstanding; and in the case of matters of faith and belief, to refuse to translate ancient words sometimes encourages nonbelief, perhaps even atheism, among those to whom the ancient words seem nonsensical.

Such, it seems to me, is the case in the petition of the Lord's Prayer on which we now focus: "Lead us not into temptation." Think about this phrase rationally rather than emotionally for a moment. If we are literal about this petition, the God to whom we pray becomes quite unbelievable. A deity who must be implored not to lead his unsuspecting people into temptation is a demonic deity. Such a phrase, if understood literally, even violates the expressed words of Holy Scripture. In the Epistle of James, the author states that no temptation comes from God (James 1:13). God tempts no one. Yet the traditional words of the Lord's Prayer seem to assume that he does because they beseech him not to do so. People, somewhat embarrassed by these words, have tried to explain them by suggesting that successfully overcoming temptation is good for us, and therefore God could be seen as deliberately leading us into temptation. But if temptation is good for us, why do we pray not to be led into it? Thus confusion abounds. One cannot help but get from these words an image of God that is mythological and anthropomorphic, a God who relates to us as dependent juveniles, a God whom we implore, beseech, and beg like infants for favors, for protection. By such a view of God many modern people are literally repelled. "If that is God, then count me out of the religion business!" is the refrain being voiced and acted out by countless people who no longer think the church has anything to say to their lives. I, for one, cannot blame them. So let us examine the words, "Lead us not into temptation," and see if they have any meaning that will make sense to our generation.

When we search the scriptures for insight, we find that the same Greek word is translated today by both "temptation" and "testing." In the modern biblical translations,* the words "tempt" and "temptation" are used only in reference to evil, never, save in the Lord's Prayer, in reference to God. In the wilderness Jesus is tempted by the devil (Matthew 4:1; Luke 4:2). In 1

* Specifically the Revised Standard Version and The New English Bible.

Corinthians Paul suggests that Satan can tempt people through lack of self-control. In 1 Timothy the author writes: "Those who want to be rich fall into temptations" (6:9). James writes in his epistle: "God is untouched by evil and tempts no man. Temptation arises when a man is lured away by his own lust. Lust conceives and gives birth to sin" (1:14). Otherwise, the word "temptation" is not used in the modern translations. Everywhere else where the older translations used the word "temptation," the modern versions employ the words "test" or "testing."

The reason for this is that the word "temptation" has for our ears an intensely moralistic sound. It is a word that we associate with sinfulness. It suggests the alcoholic feeling the lure of a bar or a gambler unable to forget the racetrack. It did not have this connotation in the original Greek. For this reason, the moralistically neuter word "test" or "testing" is suggested. There is a significant difference.

A test is that which reveals our being, our competence. Almost every experience in life is a test because it is revelatory. In our actions we reveal ourselves. Our being is seen in our capacity to give, in our ability to meet pressure or to be responsible. The real test, the ultimate revelation of our being, comes when reality strains our capacity to cope with life. When we face life's pain, life's tragedy, when we confront a bad diagnosis or the presence of death, then what we really are is seen—no masks, no role plays, no pretending. Our testing thus is finally that experience in which we know who we are and whether or not we can stand in the midst of life. The deepest test of life comes when our resources are exhausted and we have no further strength on which we can depend. Then, in biblical language we discover whether or not the Lord of life is trustworthy when he says, "Lo, I am with you always" (Matthew 28:20). No matter how intensely the winds of change blow, to know that there is an anchor to our lives, a rock on which we stand, a presence in which we live and move and find our being, a presence not affected by the passage of time or the traumas of life, is what it means not to be brought to the test.

"Lead us not into temptation" or "Do not bring us to the test" is thus a prayer which refers to this unshakable presence of God in the midst of the hard realities of life. It means "keep us so open to your love that we will not face the tests of life apart from your presence." It means "God, make your presence known to us so that we will know we are not alone in our trials. Open our eyes to see that you are nailed with us to our crosses, that you suffer with us in hurt and pain, that you die with us in our deaths." (Louis Evely) "Lead us not into temptation" means that God's great and only gift to us is to be with us, not as a heavenly parent who leads children by the hand, but as the Power of Love that calls us into being and gives us the courage to say Yes to life, come what may.

"Lead us not into temptation" means "let me know

that I am not alone." To pray this prayer is to vote for involvement in life, not withdrawal. To pray this prayer is to welcome the future rather than to dread it. It is to see every situation as an opportunity for growth and redemption. It is to view every meeting with every person as a moment for life and community. It is a prayer the world yearns to hear if we twentieth-century Christians will have the courage by deed to act it out and by word to translate it for our generation.

CHAPTER 10

God's Deliverance

➤➤➤➤➤➤ I N T H E recent history of the United States, nothing has more deeply troubled the American conscience than the armed conflict in Southeast Asia. Motives have been so mixed. The national purpose has never been clear, and a will to win has been missing. In the recent past all our ambiguities leaped into the public notice with the disclosure of the *Pentagon Papers*. It was an interesting phenomenon to watch politicians delicately attempt to maneuver around these revelations. All the misgivings about the war that were latent among Americans surfaced with a vengeance.

The *Pentagon Papers* cast doubt on our own official rationale for the war. They revealed wide discrepancy between the official public statements and the private memos of government officials. The integrity of individuals at the highest levels was called into question. For the first time many average citizens got an insight into the manner in which war is waged. They saw their nation as something less than the ideal they wanted to believe it is. They glimpsed what patriotic Americans are loath to see about their own nation—namely, that we, too, produce pure propaganda to cover our misdeeds and to blur our power plays on the world scene. They began to discern that America, like all nations and all individuals, operates from a vantage point of its own vested interest. The case can be made, of course, that throughout our history American vested interest has been the most enlightened the world has known—but it has been vested interest, nonetheless.

To those who know the story of man as portrayed in the Bible, this insight, uncomfortable as it may be, does not come as a surprise. From the story of Adam and Eve on, the Bible is a realistic book about human nature. It recognizes theologically the historic fact that all human beings are fallen, distorted, self-centered, and capable of inflicting incomparable evil on one another. We like to think we are rational, civilized, and human, but history shows us time and again a Nazi Germany, or a Czechoslovakian repression, or a Diem assassination, to keep us aware of how very thin that layer of civilization really is.

The corollary to this is also portrayed in the biblical story, namely, that not only can we do evil to one another, but we can also justify that evil to the point where we honestly believe it to be good. The American soldier in Vietnam who was quoted as saying, "The only way we could save this village was to destroy it," is a good example of this.

Other examples abound:

—Young people destroy their lives with drugs while maintaining that drugs are safe or good or chic.

—Married people practice infidelity which they justify with countless rationalizations that are so obvious we smile when we hear them outside the romantic context.

—Nations engage in a war of national self-interest and convince themselves and their people that theirs is a just cause—a holy crusade.

This is the nature of this creature, man, so capable of distortion, so easily deluded. It was Augustine who prayed, "Lord make me chaste but not yet." It was Constantine who agreed to be baptized, but postponed it until his deathbed for fear that baptism might interfere with his proposed "life style." Man's capacity to rationalize his base desires is infinite. It is this human creature, man, who is taught to pray, "Deliver us from evil"—an evil that exists nowhere except in his own distorted heart. This the Bible teaches and this life confirms.

We have found the enemy, and it is not the devil or a flaw in creation or someone strange and different. The enemy is—*ourselves.* It is from this enemy, this evil within ourselves, that we pray we may be delivered.

Where does this evil come from? As we have previously seen, deep in the heart of every man lies the insecurity of inadequate love, a distortion of being that rises from a sense of inadequacy. It is out of such negative feelings about ourselves that there comes our drive for power, for conquest, and for success, as well as our fears, our prejudices, and our bigotry. Time after time in history we human beings have ministered to our feelings of inadequacy by choosing someone else upon whom we can look down. We project our shortcomings onto the ones we elect to regard as inferior, and then we act out our self-rejection on them, somehow never seeing the contradiction. For example, prejudiced whites glibly refer to blacks as lazy and shiftless, yet strangely enough these same whites have organized society so that the blacks do the hard and menial tasks that whites are not willing to do. We brought blacks as slaves to this nation to do the physical labor that was considered beneath the white man's dignity. We even betrayed ourselves in the old days by such widely used statements as, "He works like a nigger," or "He's the laziest white man I know." Both broadcast our prejudiced feelings. It was very important to convince ourselves of the laziness of blacks so that we could avoid seeing who the lazy ones really were, so we could justify the morally indefensible role of "master." We were projecting our weakness and fear onto the victim of our prejudice. We were criticizing

another for that which we really cannot face in ourselves.

The facts of history judge us. Every nation at war is
convinced that it is acting in self-defense and that its
cause is just. The words of our national anthem are not
an accident:

"Then conquer we must, when our cause it is just,
And this be our motto, 'In God is our trust.' "

History is always written by the winners, never the
losers. It seems to weaken our position if we tolerate
doubt about our own motives; indeed, in times of national danger or stress those who express doubt about
national policy are treated as traitors. Sometimes in
fighting for freedom abroad, we destroy freedom at
home. History abounds with illustrations of the process
of projection in which a nation accuses its enemies of
the very evil which that nation is practicing.

It is our fear, our inadequacy, our insecurity, our
broken self-centeredness that the Bible calls "sin," universal and original sin. It is out of this "sin" that all human evil flows. We dump it into whatever receptacles
are available at any given moment in history. If we do
not dump it, we have to carry it ourselves and it is an
intolerable load. History has seen in progression the
persecution of Christians and Jews, Moslems, Indians,
blacks, and hippies. But always that persecution was
"justified" in the eyes of the persecutor, and inevitably
that persecution revealed far more about the persecutor

than it did about the victim. The evil of life is within the human heart. It is not in the one whom we choose to victimize.

Jesus pointed to this in the parable of the wheat and the tares. They grow together. One cannot be rooted out without destroying the other. The deepest human problem is always internal, not external, and it, like God, is inescapable. We cannot escape our evil whether we climb into the skies or sink into the depths. Nor can we escape "if we take the wings of the morning and dwell in the midst of the sea," for even there the evil in the human heart will haunt us.

How pleasant it would be if we could isolate evil and destroy it! The story is told about a preacher who felt that all the evil of life was contained in alcoholic beverages. "If all alcoholic beverages could be gathered together, all beer, wine, gin, vodka, bourbon, scotch"—I agreed with him until he listed this one—"and rum, and all could be thrown into the river, then evil," he asserted, "would be destroyed." I suppose it was the devil fighting for his life that caused that preacher then to announce that the service would conclude with the hymn "Shall We Gather by the River"!

Anyone who works with alcoholics knows that the problem is not solved when the alcohol is abandoned. The alcohol is but a symptom, a complicating symptom of the real problem which always is personal, internal, having to do with the person's being, not his doing.

It is the person who has not experienced adequate

love who feels, in the words of Thomas Harris, "not OK," who plays out his evil on the personal stage of his history. So our Lord teaches us to pray, "Deliver us from evil," which means "deliver us from the hurts, the pain, the consequences that flow out of our unloved lives."

What then delivers us? It is almost trite to say that it is love, and love alone, yet there is no other answer. It is this love which allows us to say, "I'm OK—You're OK." It is love that calls us into being; love that frees us from the need to gain power. It is love that enables us to see ourselves as we are, to see our weaknesses, our fears, our mistakes, and to face them honestly and to admit them openly. Only the life rooted in love can do that. Others must always pretend; they must cover up and hide.

Love frees us from the need to project our failures onto someone else. The loved life does not need to elect a victim to bear its prejudice, or a nation on which to exercise its power. Love gives us the courage to be what we are and to become all that we can become. Only when we know this love are we delivered from evil. "Deliver us from evil" is thus a prayer that the freeing power of love might touch us, embrace us, free us from our own distortions and fears so that we can be our real selves.

The One who taught us to pray this prayer was One who lived in this freedom that only love can bring. That is why we call him Lord and Saviour. In him we find the love and power to accept ourselves; yes, even to love ourselves. This is the first step in the process of life. To recognize that we are bound by our sense of inadequacy is to achieve some freedom from its distorting power. To know that we are loved as we are frees us to be more than we are and enables us to set others free with this same love. This is what we mean when we pray, "Deliver us from evil."

To live in the Christian experience today is to know that evil is broken even as we are victimized by it and even as we victimize others. The wheat and tares will grow together until the harvest. So even as we pray, "Deliver us from evil," we know that on this side of the kingdom, which has not fully come, we will not be fully delivered. But we can live in this world by the power of the world to come (Matthew 6:13). We can face life without despair. We can expect life to reveal the hurt, pain, prejudice, and horror that come from the heart of man, distorting history, dashing ideals, and violating humanity. We must never give up the fight; but we must also never lose hope that evil will be broken, that love is the final truth, and that whenever life-giving love is revealed in our broken world, there the God of life is seen.

First, God's love gives us the power to look inward to see what we are. Then we look outward at our community, our nation, our world to begin the serious task of praying with our lips and by our deeds, "God of love, deliver us from evil."

CHAPTER 11

God's Power Today

➤➤➤➤➤ W H E N the love of God invades human life, it is experienced as power and it reveals glory. So when we are delivered from evil, we praise the deliverer by saying, "For thine is the power."

"Power" is a fascinating word in our vocabulary. We speak of atomic power, establishment power, Black Power. We hear of power confrontations, power blocks, the power of the press, or of the pen. Political stars are born through the power of oratory, the power of charisma. Political process is established through the power of the courts or of the Presidency or of the military-industrial complex and so on for countless illustrations. What a many sided word! In many instances the word "power" evokes the feeling of fear and resentment because we might be forced to do what we do not want to do. On other occasions it is a rallying cry, a stirring affirmation, as when they cry, "Power to the people!" But what does it mean when we apply it to God? How do men discern and experience the power of God?

The history of the word "power" in religion goes back into the primitive yearnings of ancient men. At the dawn of civilization natural enemies were many. Hunger and starvation were never far removed. The mighty forces of nature kept man in fear and trembling. He felt himself to be powerless in a vast and hostile world, and out of his loneliness and his littleness he began to worship whatever he conceived to be the source of power. His was basically a religion of fear and superstition as he sought by many ritual acts to placate and gain the favor of the deity, to live in the protection of the source of power. The birth of all primitive religion was in this emotion of fear. There was little love or joy in the primitive man's worship. Power—fearful power—was the chief attribute of his god.

When we first encounter the word "power" in the Bible, it has echoes of this superstitious meaning. The power of Yahweh was seen in the affliction of Egypt with plagues (Exodus 9:16). The tales of Yahweh's power were doubtless exaggerated and spread abroad later to intimidate other enemies of the Hebrew people who quaked in fear before the members of this marauding band who were bent upon displacing the residents of Canaan.

But as the Hebrews became a settled nation, as they endured both the agony and the ecstasy of their history, the definition of the word "power," when referring to God, began to have a wider meaning. More and more God was seen as the Lord of Creation so that every created thing—man and beast, sun and moon, tree and forest—was a witness to his power (1 Chronicles 29:12). The Hebrews never identified God with nature; but whenever they looked at nature, they worshipped anew the power of God revealed through nature.* Also, they began to see God as the Lord of History. They saw his power in their victories and defeats, and in the rise and fall of every nation.† They began to refer to "the glory of his power," and in his acts of power they began to discern both justice and love.‡

When the New Testament period arrives, we find the application of the word "power" to be widened still more. Of all the Gospel writers, Luke is the one to whom this word is most appealing. He uses it more than the other Gospel writers combined. To Luke the word "power" refers to a mystical life-giving force. John the Baptist is to walk in "the power of Elijah" (Luke 1:17). Jesus is conceived when the "power of the Most High"

* Psalm 19; Jeremiah 51:55.
† Isaiah 50:2; Jeremiah 18:21; Ezekiel 35:5.
‡ Jeremiah 16:21; Daniel 2:37.

overshadows the peasant girl, Mary (1:35). Jesus comes out of the temptation experience "in the power of the Spirit" (4:14). He reveals the power to command unclean spirits and the power to heal (6:19). He possesses intrinsic power so that when a sick woman touches him, power flows out of his life and cures her (8:46). Finally, to his disciples he promises, "You will be clothed with power from on High" (24:49).

Paul expresses this New Testament meaning, for example, when he speaks of "the power of the Gospel" (Romans 1:16). The Greek word we translate as "power" is *'dunamis,'* from which we get our English word dynamite. The power of the Gospel to Paul was the power to create life, to call forth being, to maximize the human potential, to call man into all that he was created to be. This was the power of God. It was not power before which we trembled in fear, but power to which we opened ourselves in hopeful anticipation. This is the power present in the life of Jesus. When this life-giving Love confronts our lives, affirms our being, delivers us from the prison of self-centeredness, then we must pray with joy, "Thine is the power."

This is the religious history of the word "power" as used in reference to God. The power of God is seen in every movement to break chains, to reveal love, to free lives, to restore creation, to call forth in any person the image of God. The power of God is love in action; it is effective action employing redeeming power in concert with the tides of history.

We do not have to revert to superstitious fear to impress upon the modern conscience the presence of this power of God. We only need to identify it at work in places where even the skeptical, secular mind can recognize that something is happening. We must only bid secular man to look and see, experience and respond, to the power of God in our age, creating his world and calling lives into the image of their true humanity.

Look first at the revolt of the natural world. The whole created order is saying that it has a being that will not be violated forever. The natural laws of our universe have been bent so deeply that they threaten no longer to be able to sustain life. The dignity, the being of the natural world, is crying out against those who exploit creation, rape creation, and rob creation of its life. Can we not see the power of God at work there? The Creative Power behind the world, the Source of Life, is demanding to be served through his creation, not denied in the greed of men.

Look also at the stirrings among people. Throughout our world underprivileged people, powerless and exploited people, are rising to a new level of human dignity. They are proclaiming that the image of God is still writ large upon their lives, and neither slavery nor poverty nor powerlessness can deny their unique sacredness. When men think of themselves as sacred, the rest of the world can no longer regard them in any other way. The sacredness of every individual as a child of God is crying out mightily in our generation to be recognized. Can we not see the power of God at work in this? The God who is Giver of Life, the Source of Love, is demanding that he be seen in the face of every man.

Finally, there is a restlessness about modern life that is apparent to all who take the time to look. The old status symbols are empty. The success dreams of yesterday are unfulfilling. The old meanings have lost their power. People are searching today as never before for identity, for being, for freedom, for life, for love, for meaning. Without knowing it they are really searching for the biblical God. They are eager to find him, yet fearful of being deluded. Too often the "old" words or the traditional packaging simply stymie them. But when they do understand and are touched by the life-giving power of love, they glow, they shine, they dare to live. They are free to be. They meet one another in honesty. They touch. They care. They are lifted outside themselves. Can we not see the power of God at work there? He is the Creator, the Giver of Life, the Source of Love.

These are some of the places where the power of God is seen in modern life. This is the corporate manifestation of the Gospel. It is a mighty proclamation that we are not alone. God is in his world. God is in the love that calls us into life. He is in the movements of history that enhance humanity. His power is present wherever life is affirmed. Thus Paul could write: "I am not ashamed of the gospel, for the gospel is the power of God to bring salvation."

The power to live—that dynamite of life—is the final

meaning of the power of God. It is not dynamite that destroys, but dynamite that breaks us open and enables us to be all that we are meant to be. The power of God is love invading life to restore humanity to us. This is our meaning when we say in the Lord's Prayer, "For thine is the power."

CHAPTER 12

God's Glory Today

➤➤➤➤➤➤ W H E N the love of God invades life, it is experienced as power but in us it creates "glory," a glory that reveals through us the Source of Life. The life delivered from evil knows whose glory shines through him, and so he prays, "For thine is the glory."

When the Lord's Prayer was first taught to the disciples, these closing familiar words of praise were not a part of it. They were added later by a grateful church to praise the God who revealed in Christ the fullness of life—a fullness to which all who prayed his prayer were called.

The word "glory" was chosen to express these feelings because it captured a biblical truth that was deep and rich. It is worth our time to trace its development.

Our Judaeo-Christian faith was born amid the most humble of circumstances. Despite the elaborate folklore recorded in the book of Genesis, which was clearly designed to prove that the Hebrews were originally a noble people, the fact remains that our spiritual ancestors began their historic pilgrimage in the bondage of slavery (Exodus 1:8–14). How they fell into slavery is unknown. The beautiful Joseph story tries to explain the process, but it is hardly valid history (Genesis 37–50). The only historic fact of which we are certain is that when the Hebrews came to an awareness of themselves as a people, they were slaves in Egypt. They suffered the personality traits that mark all slave peoples. They were reduced upon pain of death to doing only the most menial and backbreaking physical tasks. Like all slaves, they were taught by the conquering masters that they were unfit for any higher responsibility than manual labor. Like all slaves, they were stripped of their elemental human dignity. They had their spirits broken by the system until the pain of rebellion was too great and they "knew their place." The knowledge of their previous history was systematically destroyed. Family connections were blurred. Family names and relationships were suppressed. (That is always the process of slavery in history. The neurosis is complete when the slaves no longer overtly question their lot as slaves, no longer rebel, no longer resent openly the radical injustice of their plight.) This was the picture of the Hebrew people in Egypt, the folk in whom our religious heritage was born.

Yet the hope of freedom continued to flicker among these people, if only in an underground way. They developed songs, folklore, mythology, and dreams from which no lash of the taskmaster could ever separate them. Finally came the day, as it always does, when the slave people escaped their bondage. History's man-of-the-moment was Moses. Though part Hebrew by birth, Moses was raised as an Egyptian prince. Yet he deliberately chose to identify himself with the slave people. He was a man who felt the indignities of the Hebrews, who bore their oppression, and whose moral sensitivity was offended at their plight. He decided he would share their slavery and bear their pain. It is hard for us to over-estimate what that moment meant to the Hebrews. A nation of slaves, a people taught that they were without worth or value—in their own eyes nobodies, oppressed, hated, regarded as fit only for servitude; and yet this noble man chose to cast his lot with them. It was doubt-less out of this experience that they felt themselves to be a chosen people, an elected folk, a favored nation, not just in the eyes of Moses but also in the eyes of the God Yahweh about whom Moses taught them. To be the people of Yahweh was not to be in slavery, but instead, to be a nation of destiny, a holy folk. It is no wonder that the sense of pride among the Hebrews was rooted solely in their worship. It is no wonder that when they spoke of "the glory of Israel," they meant neither wealth nor conquest nor military might, but rather the presence of God in their midst. It was this presence of God that called them into being and gave this people, who had been nobodies, their pride, their worth, their dignity. When the Ark of the Lord was stolen from the Hebrews, they referred to this as "the glory of God departing from Israel" (1 Samuel 4:21). The glory of God to the Hebrews was always the presence of God in the midst of their life, whether symbolized by the cloud, the fiery pillar, or the Ark. The more Israel fulfilled her destiny, the more God's glory was seen.

The glory of God was also seen by the Hebrews when that glory was reflected in the life of God's people. Its brightness could never be viewed at its primary source, for even the holy man, Moses, could never see God face to face (Exodus 33:18). The Hebrews searched for other synonyms to refer to God's presence in their life. They spoke of his splendor, his pomp, his wealth, his honor; but finally the word "glory" was their favorite, and they used it over and over. When their life and purpose, their dignity and being, were revealed in their history, what Israel saw was "the glory of God." Hence the psalmist cries, "Thou, O God, art my glory" (Psalm 89:17). The psalmist refers to man who is "crowned with God's glory" (8:5), and to Israel's worship as the place "where God's glory dwells" (26:8).

The passionate resistance in the Old Testament to

idolatry is rooted in this understanding of God's glory.
If a Hebrew worshipped anything other than God, he
lost that which set him apart, that in which his value
was grounded, that which was his glory—he lost that
which gave him his life. The more alive men were, the
more the glory of God was seen in them. This was the
Old Testament understanding of the glory of God,
which had been born out of the history of a slave people
chosen to come alive to their destiny as the people of
God.

It is against this background that the New Testament
writers could proclaim the Christ story, for it is the story
of the totally alive man whose life revealed that he had
come "in the glory of the Father" (John 8:54). It is of
the birth of Jesus that Luke could write: "The glory of
the Lord shone round about" (2:9), and he portrayed the
shepherds and the angels singing, "Glory to God" (2:14).
Of him John could write: "We beheld his glory"; that
is, we saw him fully alive in "the glory of the only be-
gotten Son of God, full of grace and truth" (John 1:14).
And in the high priest prayer of the Fourth Gospel account of the Last Supper, Jesus prays, "Father, glorify
the son with the glory I had with thee" (17:5)—that is,
reveal in me the fullness of life, for the fullness of life
portrays the glory of God. But it is finally the Apostle
Paul who fills the word "glory" with its richness. True
to the biblical tradition, the glory of God for Paul refers
to God's reflection in human life, a reflection that is seen
in man's true being, his essential character, his destiny,

or what man was meant to be. Sin distorts the glory of God in us, Paul asserts (Romans 3:23). The glory of God is seen by Paul when the power of love breaks the power of sin and frees us to accept what we are, to love what we are, and to be what we are. The glory of God is seen when we are so affirmed and fulfilled that we do not feel the need to glorify ourselves any longer (Romans 1:23), when we are free to give and to share and to love without worrying about our image. It is in this experience, Paul argues, that we find the power of the Gospel. Hence Paul preaches that when God's loving presence breaks the power of sin in us and frees us to be our true selves, then the glory of God is revealed in our lives (Romans 8:18).

Irenaeus, a Christian theologian writing in the year A.D. 175, captured this meaning when he wrote: "The glory of God is man fully alive." When you and I are alive to all of our potentialities, then men will see in us the glory of God. This is the biblical definition of this great word. When we grasp this definition, then we understand why men could say of the totally alive Jesus, he comes "in the glory of the Father." Then we know what our purpose is as the church of Christ in this world, namely, to reveal the glory of God by living and loving, and through our loving lives, calling men to be what they were created to be. We are to be the Body of Christ to the world as love working through our lives brings us freedom, the capacity to care, to give, and to share.

All of this lies behind that final phrase in the Lord's

Prayer, "for thine is the glory." We glorify God, the
Source of Life, the Ground of Being, when we live in
the fullness of life and become agents of that life to our
world and share it with every one of God's children. Let
us live, then, so that our lives shout to highest heaven,
"For thine is the glory!"

CHAPTER 13

The Amen of Honest Prayer

→>>>→>>> W H A T , then, is prayer?

OUR FATHER

It is life that acknowledges the all-giving Father by being the responsible and giving son.

WHO ART IN HEAVEN

It is the recognition that heaven, the abode of God, is wherever the love of God lifts us out of our prisons and restores us to him, to each other, and to ourselves.

HALLOWED BE THY NAME

It is the ability to see that keeping holy the name of God is done by becoming our deepest and truest selves.

THY KINGDOM COME

It is the recognition that the kingdom of God comes when love is shared, but that it will never come completely until love is total.

THY WILL BE DONE

It is to live in this world in joyful but discontented hope. It is to live by the power of the world to come, which we have but tasted.

GIVE US THIS DAY OUR DAILY BREAD

It is to see that to pray for the will of God to come on earth is to make a commitment to be actively and passionately involved in the affairs of life, including a commitment to share our life, our humanity, and our bread with every child of God.

FORGIVE US AS WE FORGIVE

It is to know that our loneliness is shared by everyone so that once we have tasted love, acceptance, and forgiveness, we will be compelled to share it by loving, accepting, and forgiving in our turn.

LEAD US NOT INTO TEMPTATION

It is to experience life so deeply that we face life's crises and tests with confidence, knowing that nothing will destroy us, for nothing can separate us from the Source of Life.

DELIVER US FROM EVIL

It is to recognize that evil always starts in the brokenness of our inner lives and that only love can deliver us.

THINE IS THE POWER

It is to know that the love that delivers us is experienced by us as power and revealed in us as glory.

THINE IS THE GLORY

It is to rejoice with the insight of Irenaeus that "the glory of God is man fully alive."

That is prayer.

Prayer is that state of life in which Paul exhorts us to participate without ceasing. It is life-centered, involved, and very real.

To pray is a disciplined exercise preparing us to live. It is the bringing to conscious thought the fears, the concerns, the confessions, the thanksgivings of our life. It is the opening of ourselves to the deepening meanings of God. It is the daily reminder that the God we meet in life, in history, in one another is the only presence that we confront here; but outside this confrontation, he is infinite, incomprehensible, and transcendent power beyond our capability of imagining. He calls us to live; and when we do, we meet him. When we meet him and know him, we cannot help but share him.

Honest prayer requires that we be willing to throw ourselves into life with joy, exhausting each precious moment of all its wonderment by scaling its heights and plumbing its depths. Honest prayer involves the worship of that living power that is revealed in every event of history and in every relationship. Honest prayer demands a willingness to live with daring, courageous abandon. Honest prayer is not for the timid, it is for the bold. Be *bold* then and *honest* and say, "Our Father."

Amen. May it be so.

SOME HELPFUL BOOKS

Pierre Teilhard de Chardin: *How I Believe*. New York: Harper and Row, 1969.

Jacques Ellul: *Prayer and Modern Man*. New York: Seabury Press, 1970.

Louis Evely: *Our Prayer*. New York: Herder and Herder (McGraw Hill), 1970.
The Prayer of a Modern Man. New Jersey: Dimension Books, 1968.

Joachim Jeremias: *The Lord's Prayer, Biblical Series*. Philadelphia: Fortress Press, 1964.

Paul Tillich: *The Eternal Now*. New York: Scribners,
    1963.
    The New Being. New York: Scribners, 1965.

John Youngblut: *Rediscovering Prayer*. New York: Sea-
    bury Press, 1972.